PRODUCT SAFETY MANAGEMENT GUIDELINES

SECOND EDITION

National
Safety
Council

PRODUCT SAFETY MANAGEMENT GUIDELINES

SECOND EDITION

WARNING

CAUTION

DANGER

Project Leader: Patricia M. Laing
Technical Advisor: J. Terrence Grisim, CSP, CDS, CPSM, ARM, Chairman,
Product Safety Committee and Chairman of the review committee

Written by a subcommittee of the Product Safety Standing Committee
of the Business and Industry Division of the National Safety Council.

Disclaimer
Although the information and recommendations contained in this publication have
been compiled from sources believed to be reliable, the National Safety Council makes
no guarantee as to, and assumes no responsibility for, the correctness, sufficiency, or
completeness of such information or recommendations. Other or additional safety
measures may be required under particular circumstances.

National Safety Council Mission Statement
**The mission of the National Safety Council is to educate and influence society
to adopt safety, health, and environmental policies, practices, and procedures
that prevent and mitigate human suffering and economic losses arising from
preventable causes.**

Library of Congress Cataloging-in-Publication Data
National Safety Council. Product Safety Committee.
      Product safety management guidelines / [written by a subcommittee
of the Product Safety Standing Committee of the Business and Industry Division
of the National Safety Council]. — 2nd ed.
          p.   cm.
      Includes bibliographical references and index.
      ISBN-13: 978-0-87912-193-8
      1. Product safety—Management. I. Title.
TS175.N37 1996
658.5'6—DC20   96-42201
                                                                    CIP

2.5C0906   Product Number: 17655-0000

Contents

Preface

Unintentional injuries, including unintentional fatalities, occur at
a rate of over 18.7 million per year in the United States—affecting
1 out of 14 persons in the population. Considering that many unintentional injuries and deaths involve one or more products, it becomes
clear that few companies face absolutely no product safety problems.

Most retailers, wholesalers, and manufacturers of products and
subassemblies have adopted a strong concern about the safety and
health of the people who use or consume their products. They are
taking extra steps to prevent injury and/or illness to consumers or
damage to the environment. Some of these steps include:

- Formulating strong policies aimed at protecting product users

- Creating and maintaining a Product Safety Department to
  monitor their products

- Complying with standards far more stringent than the
  governmental requirements

- Taking extra care to educate the consumer through product
  literature and advertising

- Stressing to employees that a product safety problem is
  everyone's problem

At the same time, the rising costs of legal claims and damage awards
have created a product liability crisis in the United States. Ultimately,
companies pass on their increased costs to the consumer. Liability
expenses can result from payment of claims, verdicts, judgments, settle-
ments, legal fees, investigative costs, expert fees, and perhaps punitive
damage awards. There are also corollary costs, such as increased insurance premiums; advertising and public relations efforts to counteract

adverse publicity; recall campaigns; lost time of corporate management, legal personnel, and technical personnel; restriction of research and development; and corporate wariness that leads to defensive decision-making (particularly concerning introducing certain new products and applying new technology or innovative ideas).

Customer satisfaction is another reason to promote product safety efforts. A recent college textbook, in describing consumerism, presented the author's idea of "the right to safety." One idea was that "society expects marketing organizations not to knowingly sell any products that could result in personal injury or harm, and it wants unsafe products modified or removed from the market." (Steven J. Skinner, *Marketing*, Boston: Houghton Mifflin Company, 1990.) From such a viewpoint, even the most prosaic products, such as concrete bricks, hammers, peanut butter, and books, would have to be banned. It is not reasonable to try to remove all risks from the world, but this viewpoint illustrates the direction in which societal expectations are moving.

In the phrase "prevent and mitigate human and economic losses," the National Safety Council recognizes in its mission statement that in an imperfect world, there will always be risks (see Mission Statement in the front of this book). Making safety a necessary criteria for products does not entail striving for the impossible—zero risk. Rather, product safety requires a strong concern for safety in all aspects of a product so that unnecessary risks can be eliminated.

PURPOSE AND SCOPE

The purpose of this book is to assist those who provide products to develop internal procedures for the safe design, manufacture, distribution, and use of those products. The material also serves as a valuable reference to line supervisors, design engineers, and legal and insurance specialists. Indeed, anyone involved in the training of manufacturing, quality assurance, and sales personnel will find essential information on how to communicate product safety awareness.

Product Safety Management Guidelines is for those who have been given or share the responsibility for product safety within their organization. This book covers the basics of how to set up a new product safety department, but does not attempt to supply technical expertise in specific areas. Discussions and definitions are guided by current law and case findings. However, for detailed governmental regulations and legal case histories, readers should consult other sources. Some major sources are listed in the References at the end of this book.

These guidelines will assist the product safety professional in:

- Identifying the key elements in an effective product safety program

- Discussing what to do first to establish and/or maintain a product safety program

- Discussing the sources of loss due to product-related accidents

- Discussing how to control or minimize such losses

- Listing the programs and information sources available to help the product safety professional maintain and augment the product safety program in his or her organization

- Exploring every department's product safety responsibilities

Product Safety Management Guidelines will alert and inform the reader about the appropriate concerns of those involved in product safety. The recommendations and opinions in this book are the result of the consensus of informed specialists. However, there are many differences of opinion on legal definitions, applicable law in a given jurisdiction, engineering knowledge, and technical devices. Readers should consult with a specialist in the appropriate field before taking any action related to product safety matters.

The National Safety Council extends a special thank you to the following members of the Product Safety Standing Committee and contributors who devoted many hours to researching, revising, and proofreading this edition of *Product Safety Management Guidelines*:

Review Committee Chairman:
J. Terrence Grisim,
CSP, CDS, CPSM, ARM

Review Committee Members:

Roger L. Andrews   Campbell G. Dewey, CSP
Roger F. Borghesani   Gordon L. Leach
Edward D. Bullard   Douglas L. Sten, MSSM, CSP
Kaz Darzinskis

We also thank Catherine M. Thorsen, of the U.S. Consumer Products Safety Commission, for her assistance in revising Appendix 2, Key Elements of the Consumer Product Safety Act.

1 Basic Concepts

Where there are people, there are products—from the busiest metropolis to the most remote wilderness community. In their myriad forms, products can make our lives longer, healthier, and more productive, prosperous, and comfortable than anyone could have imagined just a few generations ago.

On the negative side, however, a majority of accidental injuries or deaths occurring today are associated with at least one or more products. People usually associate product injuries with extremely hazardous products or activities, such as those requiring the use of parachutes, explosives, and nuclear materials. However, injuries from familiar products such as hammers, safety pins, stepladders, and bicycles are reported by hospitals far more often than are injuries from unfamiliar, "exotic," or dangerous items.

Contrary to popular belief, most accidents involving users are not caused by a malfunction or an unsafe characteristic of a product. Accidents typically involve multiple factors—people's behavior, the environment in which products are used, and the performance of the products. In fact, human behavior and environmental conditions each trigger or are associated with more accidents than are product failures. Thus, accidents are generally caused by a combination of factors, not simply one blameworthy "cause" related to the product, user, or environment.

Multinational organizations also are becoming more aware of worldwide product safety requirements. For example, European Union member states are required to establish, on a community level, a general safety requirement for any product placed on the market that is intended for consumers or likely to be used by consumers. Furthermore, manufacturers and others must supply consumers with product information, inform consumers of the risks that these products might present, and adopt safety measures commensurate with the characteristics of the products. These requirements are stated in the Council of European Communities Directive 92/59/EEC of June 29, 1992:

> *Whereas* it is therefore necessary to establish on a Community level a general safety requirement for any product placed on the market that is intended for consumers or likely to be used by consumers;

> *Whereas* it is appropriate to supplement the duty to observe the general safety requirement by an obligation on economic operators to supply consumers with relevant information and adopt measures commensurate with the characteristics of the products, enabling them to be informed of the risks that these products might present.

SOURCES OF LOSSES

Product safety issues are a potential problem for all organizations involved in placing a product in the stream of commerce, selling it, servicing it, or disposing of it. Incidents or accidents may arise from any one or a combination of the following business activities:

- Product concept
- Research
- Design
- Development
- Testing
- Manufacturing
- Quality assurance
- Noncompliance with industry standards, regulations, codes, and customary practices
- Warnings, instructions, and information
- Advertising and representations
- Marketing and sales
- Maintenance, service, and repairs
- Packaging, shipping, storage, and handling

- Recall, modification, product improvement (after sale)

- Refurbishing, remanufacture

- Disposal and destruction

As a result, product safety concerns are not limited to manufacturers but can be critical issues for wholesalers, distributors, retailers, service and repair organizations, and various contracting firms. A 1988 survey conducted by the Conference Board (an independent, nonprofit business research organization) revealed that about 40% of the surveyed CEOs reported that the threat of product liability litigation had a major impact on their firms. About 36% said they had discontinued product lines, 15% had laid off workers, and 8% had closed down plants as a result of product liability litigation. (*Industry Week*, 1988) Others had modified their products or found market opportunities for their products, programs, or services that were better positioned in terms of product liability prevention, mitigation, avoidance, or risk reduction.

BASIC DEFINITIONS

To be prepared for potential complaints and to know how to respond to them, a company must thoroughly understand all possible bases for claims. The following definitions may help to clarify where product safety could be jeopardized in the manufacture and use (or even misuse) of products, and what might be a potential source of loss for an organization. A detailed discussion of the law or lawsuits is not within the scope of this book, but there are several publications cited in the References that do discuss the legal reasoning and case histories behind the following definitions. (See also Chapter 10, Risk Management, and the Appendix 5, Glossary.)

Product

A product can be a consumer, industrial, or professional product and can include the following:

- The specific item sold

- The sales literature, labels, manuals, and advertising supplied with the item, attached to it, printed on it, or printed or sent separately after purchase

- The parts, equipment, accessories, and special tools supplied by the manufacturer to the customer (Figure 1–1)

Figure 1–1.
The pallet contains a product, including an Owner/Operator Manual, ready to be shipped to the buyer/user.

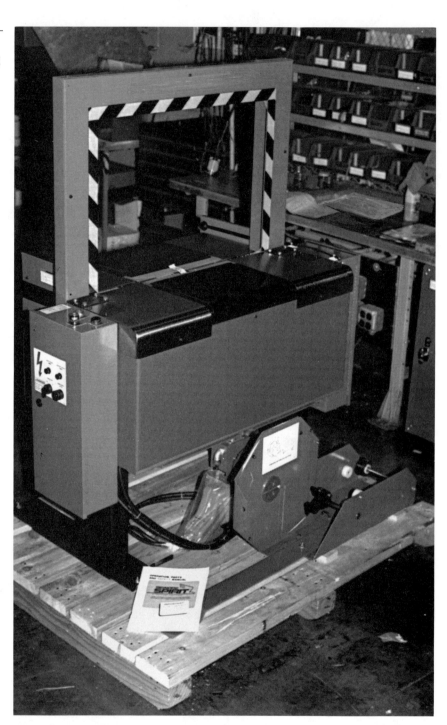

The environment in which the product is installed may also be an influence in defining the item. For example, a product may include a large gas or steam turbine, the fuels and lubricants that make it work, and the nuts and bolts that hold it together. Any special installation tools, such as a wrench, are also considered part of the product. (See Appendix 1, Product Safety and Real Property, for a discussion of real property as a product.) Finally, a product is generally not considered a product until it has been sold to a user or consumer. It is also considered "sold" if it has been rented, leased, loaned, given as a free sample, or used for demonstration. Once a product has been sold, it is a potential source of legal liability for the manufacturer or anyone in the chain of distribution if it is involved in an accident. Anyone distributing, reselling, installing, or servicing a product may be held liable in a number of ways.

Negligence

Negligence (in a product liability context) is the failure to carefully design, assemble, inspect, test, package, ship, and handle products, resulting in a product-related injury. It is the manufacturer's duty to ensure that the product presents no unreasonable risk of injury. The manufacturer's performance of this duty is measured against what a "reasonable man of ordinary prudence" would have done. A reasonable person is one who acts in the ordinary or usual way; one whose actions are suitable, fit, and appropriate to the end in view. (Black, 1993) (The "reasonable man" doctrine applies only to negligence issues.) The manufacturer may be found negligent in failing to fulfill this legal duty in the manufacture or design of a product, including failure to supply adequate instructions, warnings, and packaging.

Those who handle a product after its manufacture also have legal duties which, if violated or ignored, could lead to findings of negligence. For example, wholesalers, distributors, and repackagers generally have a duty to pass along to buyers any product warnings provided by the manufacturer. Retailers have a duty to accurately portray the safety features of a product to customers. Negligence laws apply in all 50 of the United States. Products marketed overseas may have to conform to similar legal requirements. Negligence applies to both products and services. (See Chapter 3, Product Design and Evaluation, for a discussion of European regulations.)

Strict Liability

Strict liability is the imposition of liability for damages without requiring proof of negligence. The issue in a strict liability case is whether the product is legally defective when it leaves the care, custody, and control of the manufacturer. "Defective" does not necessarily mean, as it does in common understanding, that the product obviously fails to work, malfunctions, fractures, or falls apart. It means defective in terms of design, warnings, safety, consumer expectations of product performance, or some other legal definition peculiar to a state or other jurisdiction. In some states, a product is legally defective if a jury considers it unreasonably dangerous. (Weinstein, 1978) According to W.L. Prosser, "The prevailing interpretation of 'defective' is that the product does not meet the reasonable expectations of the ordinary consumer as to its safety." (*Handbook of the Law of Torts*, 1971) Nearly every state has some form of strict liability law. (Strict liability generally does not apply to services.)

In practical terms, a product may be "defective" under strict liability:

- If an alternative existed to the design, function, assembly, or part of the product

- If that alternative would have eliminated or prevented the injury

- If that alternative was economically feasible and would not cause other safety or performance problems. Consequently, the manufacturer may be held strictly liable for any injury or property damage caused by the product.

In some jurisdictions, the manufacturer is presumed to have had knowledge of the hazards and unsafe characteristics of the product (whether or not the individual actually knows) when the product was first manufactured, if the hazards could have become known to the manufacturer as an "expert" in the field through reading the literature, research, testing, or technical analyses. The issue is often whether a manufacturer or seller would have sold the product or put it into the chain of distribution knowing the potential hazards associated with it. Many products (such as automobiles, machine tools, snowmobiles, cranes, and pharmaceuticals) were alleged to be unreasonably dangerous, unsafe, or defective when it became known that safer alternative designs existed.

Warranty Law

A warranty is an implied or expressed promise regarding the performance and characteristics of a product. In the context of product liability, a warranty is an implied or expressed promise that the product is reasonably safe for its intended use. In a product liability lawsuit based upon a warranty, the issue is generally whether the product failed to meet its expressed or implied guarantees of merchantability and fitness of purpose.

These concepts have been expanded by case law, perhaps beyond their original meaning, to include the concept that buyers of products are entitled to have certain reasonable safe-use expectations fulfilled. This is why product safety professionals must be especially careful about what safety capabilities are implied or explicitly claimed in any labels, literature, statements, or advertisements about a product. A verbal statement made by a salesperson could become the basis of a warranty claim. Although some "puffing," or exaggeration, by a salesperson is legally permitted, this is an area where legal guidance is necessary. (See also Chapter 4, Product Communications Design.)

INFORMATION SOURCES

According to an old saying, nothing is known about a subject until numbers are attached to it. Whether or not this is true, one of the first things a newly assigned product safety professional should do is to examine any and all historical data regarding the number, type, and circumstances of past accidents and incidents involving the company's products. Such data should include both property damage as well as bodily injury accidents, and both minor and serious accidents. If the company's products contain potentially hazardous materials of any kind, the safety professional should obtain all data concerning theoretical and actual health ramifications to users. Companies should seek the recommendations of legal counsel about how long to retain historical safety and accident data. (See also Chapter 8, Record Retention Requirements.) This section discusses both internal and external sources of product safety data.

Internal Data Sources

Internal company sources frequently have the best, most relevant data to be found. Even if no one has been "officially" responsible for collecting such information in the past, there probably are some employees who have recorded at least part of the story. These employees might include whatever group receives or handles warranty claims, whether the group is in sales, quality control, field service, or design engineering. "Field information"—data from field service, sales, and repair departments—is particularly valuable because these departments are closest to the product user. In addition, the legal and risk management departments are likely to have files or computer printouts on any serious injury claims, investigations, or other reports.

If an effective system for gathering such data does not exist, establishing one should be a high priority. One system through which a manufacturer can attempt to predict accidents with products (even when few or no accidents have occurred) is brainstorming in groups. The approach includes selecting representatives from design, manufacturing, field service, marketing, insurance, and so on to brainstorm new products. Once the attendees have been given a short overview of how product claims are pursued, there is usually enough in-house expertise to visualize how future accidents involving these new products could happen. The group would need to know the history of accidents involving similar products to predict the number and types of accidents involving the new items.

The approach could involve creating committees of three or four people, with at least two groups per product. The committee guidelines generally would include identifying the problem, but not prescribing a complete solution. Later in the committee meeting, the group might establish company priorities and set target dates for corrective action regarding product-related incidents.

The Consumer Product Safety Act and some governmental agencies require that companies report certain types of accidents to the Consumer Product Safety Commission (CPSC). (See Appendix 2, Key Elements of the Consumer Product Safety Act.)

External Data Sources

The occupational safety professional, industrial hygienist, or medical personnel at a facility that uses a company's product(s) also may be able to supply data on past accidents and incidents. To place a company's accident data in the context of industry, state, or federal statistics, external data sources should be tapped. These sources provide insight into user accidents, including behavior associated with particular classes of products that may include the company's products and those of one or more competitors. If the products are sold through independent dealers, there may be a way to tie in with the dealers' data collection systems.

Consumer Products

With regard to consumer products, the largest data base recording product injuries is the National Electronic Injury Surveillance System (NEISS) statistics. (NEISS receives injury reports from 119 hospitals on product-related injuries in which victims were given emergency room treatment. These 119 hospitals are a representative sample for the continental United States and account for an estimated 38% of all product-related injury reports. Since May 14, 1973, NEISS has been the primary tool of the Consumer Product Safety Commission for collecting statistical injury data upon which the CPSC can form their policies and operational decisions. This data base, gathered and maintained by the CPSC, is an ongoing information-gathering system using hospital emergency room admissions. (See Appendix 3, Injuries Associated with Consumer Products.) Data are published in annual reports available to anyone who requests them. CPSC also does in-depth causal investigations for some products involved in accidents, such as portable kerosene heaters. (Call the local or national CPSC office for further information.)

Industrial Products

No nationwide accident reporting data base exists for industrial products used in the workplace. There are alternative data sources, however, from which companies and individuals can obtain inferential accident statistics. The U.S. Department of Labor maintains the Supplementary Data System (SDS), which compiles standardized morbidity ratios from workers' compensation census data. These data have been collected from 33 states since 1976. The reports of injuries or illnesses submitted by employers and insurance carriers to state workers' compensation agencies include the age, sex, and nature of injury. Federal and, in some states, self-employed workers are not included.

The Department of Labor, Bureau of Labor Statistics (BLS) has done a number of surveys of workplace accidents classified by type of employer. The National Safety Council publishes *International Accident Facts*, 1995, and *Accident Facts*, annually. In addition, some industries and industry associations publish workplace accident data for their own industry. NIOSH also publishes accident statistics in certain industries, such as printing. (See References for addresses.)

Another external source of accident statistics might be the associations relevant to industrial or mercantile products. Consult the *Encyclopedia of Associations* for particular associations.

Insurance companies collect accident data for various classifications of both products and workplaces. Some insurance companies have safety specialists who will help gather and analyze data or provide advice based on their past claims experience.

Industry-specific consultants, periodicals, newsletters, and trade magazines might supply valuable information and statistics. Most common among the latter are the *Personal Injury Newsletter*, *Product Liability Letter*, and *Products Liability Reports*.

Safety libraries and bibliographies are maintained by several organizations. For example, the National Safety Council maintains an in-house data base available for public use. Information is also available from the National Fire Protection Association (NFPA).

Professional products are those intended for use by professionals rather than by the general public (i.e., retail consumers). These products usually are sold to professionals, such as medical practitioners, clinics or laboratories, lawyers, and so on, or to corporate users of business products. Professional products may have higher standards for reliability and safety, depending on the customer needs and whether they are used in a workplace that must adhere to federal, state, or local regulations. In addition, these products may need to be biodegradable, or otherwise harmless to the environment, and recyclable.

The local public library system can also provide the product safety professional with the data needed for use in accident prevention, systems preventive measures, and litigation defense. Check with the reference librarian for help in locating or using the following sources:

Periodicals

Keywords to use for search strategies:

Product(s)—Accident

Product(s)—Consumers

Product(s)—Design

Product(s)—Labels, Labeling

Product(s)—Liability

Product(s)—Safety

Product(s)—Signs

Product(s)—Warnings

1. *Readers' Guide to Periodical Literature*

2. *Business Periodical Index*

3. *Applied Science and Technology Index*

4. *Biological and Agricultural Index*

5. *Engineering Index (Dialog File 8—Compendex)*

6. *Social Sciences Index*

7. *Psychological Abstracts (Dialog File 11—Psychinfo)*

8. *Index Medicus (Dialog Files 152, 153, 154—Medline)*

9. *Union List of Periodicals*

Books

1. *Computer search subject listings*

2. *Books in Print*

Computer Data Bases

1. Dialog Information Retrieval Service

2. National Technical Information Service publications can be searched via File 6 NTIS. Check NTIS list of already published searches in a particular area of interest.

3. *Magazine Index* (File 47)

4. Highway safety and related topics can be reached via File 63 TRIS.

5. *Comprehensive Dissertation Index* (File 35)

6. *National Agriculture Library* (Files 10 and 110 AGRICOLA)

7. *Standards and Specifications* (File 113)

8. *Dialog Database Catalog*

9. *Encyclopedia of Information Systems and Services*

10. *Computer Readable Databases*

11. *Lexis Database*

Professional and Trade Associations

1. Periodicals and books they publish

2. Product liability prevention programs for member companies

References

1. *Encyclopedia of Associations* (Dialog File 14)

2. *Directory of Directories*

3. *Bibliographic Index*

4. *Statistics Sources*

5. *Information USA*

Law Libraries

1. Global Engineering Documents 1–800–854–7179
7730 Corondeleo Avenue
Suite 407
Clayton, MO 63105

2. UNIPUB 1–800–274–4888
4611–F Assembly Drive
Lanham, MD 20706–4391

3. CEEM Information Service Report 1–800–745–5565
(i.e., EC Product Liability & Product Safety Directives)
10521 Braddock Road
Fairfax, VA 22032–2236

4. The EC Machinery Directive has been implemented in United
Kingdom law by the Supply of Machinery (Safety) Regulations 1992
(SI 1992/3073) and the Supply of Machinery (Safety) (Amendment)
Regulations 1994 (SI 1994/2063). Copies of the Regulations are available from HMSO bookshops and accredited agents or from the HMSO
Publications Centre on 0171 873 9090 or fax: 0171 873 8200.

5. The DTI booklet *Product Standards—Machinery (May 1995)* gives
comprehensive information on the Supply of Machinery (Safety)
Regulations 1992 (as amended) and a broad range of contacts for
further information. The booklet is available from the DTI's Business
in Europe Hotline on 0117 944 4888.

REFERENCES

Black, HC. *Black's Law Dictionary*, 6th ed. St. Paul: West Publishing
Company, 1993.

Handbook of the Law of Torts, 4th edition, St. Paul: West Publishing
Company, 1971, p. 659.

Industry Week, May 2, 1988, p. 6.

Weinstein, AS et al. *Products Liability and the Reasonably Safe Product: A
Guide for Management, Design, and Marketing.* New York: John Wiley
and Sons, 1978.

2 Product Safety Program

A good product safety program requires a corporate policy statement, clear objectives, committed leadership, effective organizational systems, knowledgeable personnel, a specific program, employee involvement and awareness, and individual support at all levels. The International Organization for Standardization (ISO) audit process described in ISO 9000 includes five elements: (1) a policy statement, (2) roles and responsibilities, (3) written procedures, (4) practices, and (5) training. This chapter discusses ways that a company can achieve such leadership, organization, and involvement. It covers not only management structures but also ways to increase employee awareness of product safety as it affects each individual's job and the final user. Increasing safety awareness can be accomplished, in part, through the employee training techniques discussed in this chapter.

PROGRAM LEADERSHIP

Top management establishes leadership for product safety by:

- Setting product safety as an important business objective

- Providing the resources (human, technical, and financial) to identify goals and shortcomings

- Providing ready and willing access to persons who could or should identify a product safety problem

- Taking considered reasonable action where necessary, either directly or by delegating specific responsibility and authority

How these four steps are conceived and accomplished may vary, particularly in terms of how formally they are implemented. Management should avoid prescribing any one set of procedures or practices for the organization. However, those setting up a product safety program or those auditing, monitoring, or reevaluating an existing one will benefit from knowing, in general, how corporations across the country provide leadership for the product safety function. Companies of any size will find useful guidelines in the following organizational overview. The product safety program should have an important place within the organizational structure. The components of the program can include the policy statement, procedures manuals, safety committees, and a product safety professional.

Product Safety Policy Statement

The content of a written product safety policy statement varies with the philosophy and size of the company. The objective of a policy statement is to communicate the company's ideals and product safety commitment to the employees. It may contain only policy issues, or it may also include general procedures, objectives, assignments, and even individual responsibilities. (Figure 2–1.) Company policy statements may contain some or all of the following elements:

- A statement of the company's intent to produce and market products that are reliable and safe for the user and the environment

- A statement of the company's intent to comply with all applicable federal, state, and local product safety regulations

- A statement that the company will use all reasonable means to eliminate or minimize all potential hazards related to the development, manufacturing, distribution, and use of its products

- The identification of the Corporate Product Safety Professional by name or title and the person to whom the safety professional reports

- A detailed list of objectives or goals, including specific product safety responsibilities, organizational descriptions, and administrative procedures for implementing the policy

- Specific goals for reduction in claims, customer complaints, returned goods, scrap, recall, government agency penalties, failures of product, rework, and accidents or incidents

- Other considerations such as continuous improvement and environmentally safe recycling or disposal

Figure 2–1.
This sample product safety policy statement covers all operations of the corporation.

Product Safety Policy

It is the policy of _____ to design, manufacture, and distribute all products and to handle and dispose of all materials safely without creating unacceptable risks to health, safety, or the environment. The organization will:

- Establish and maintain programs to ensure that laws and regulations applicable to its products and operations are known and followed.

- Adopt its own standards where laws or regulations may not be adequately protective, and adopt, where necessary, its own standards where laws do not exist.

- Stop manufacturing or distributing any product or carrying out any operation if the health, safety, or environmental risks are unacceptable.

To carry out this policy, the organization will:

- Identify and control public health, safety, and environmental hazards stemming from its operations and products.

- Conduct accident prevention, product safety and integrity, occupational health, and pollution control programs to safeguard employees and the public from injuries or health hazards, to protect the organization's assets and continuity of operations, and to protect the environment.

- Conduct and support appropriate research regarding the health, safety, and environmental effects of materials and products handled and sold by the organization and share promptly any significant findings with others, such as employees, suppliers, customers, government agencies, or the scientific community.

- Conduct work constructively with trade associations, governmental agencies, and others to develop equitable and realistic laws, regulations, and standards to protect public health, safety, and the environment.

Every employee is expected to adhere to the spirit as well as the letter of this policy. Managers have a special obligation to keep informed about health, safety, and environmental risks and standards and to advise top management promptly of any adverse situation which comes to their attention.

Chairman of the Board
Chief Executive Officer

The Corporate Product Safety Policy Statement should be communicated to all appropriate employees. It should be included, in part or in whole, in guides and manuals for supervisors and executive personnel. It may be supplemented by policy statements from divisional or operating unit executives.

Policy Statement Objectives

When effectively implemented, the influence and results of a formal product safety statement can be profound. In one respect, it simply documents the company's intent to meet both its legal and ethical obligations toward its workers, its customers, and the society in which it functions. But the safety statement also serves as a warning to managers and employees that violations of product safety standards will not be tolerated. It provides common goals and promotes communication among departments, thus enhancing company efforts to produce safe, reliable products. It helps prevent oversight or neglect of the product safety function.

Other ways in which management can demonstrate its commitment to product safety include:

- Safety meetings (scheduled or informal)
- Posted bulletins and notices in newsletters
- Meetings (similar to safety tailgate meetings)
- Distribution of brochures and safety-related information
- Special mailings to employees

Product Safety Professional

When a company designates a person or department to manage product safety activities, the responsibility is usually one of a number of functions that designees perform. When management decides to make the product safety professional position part time, the responsibility often falls on the quality control or engineering department. The organizational assignment depends on the personnel available, the nature of the organization, and the types of products made. Product safety activities are more often only part of the designated person's duties rather than the individual's full-time duties. Some portion of the product safety function is often assigned to other departments, depending upon the complexity, needs, and personal talents involved in the organization. These departments include insurance, marketing, legal, occupational safety, industrial hygiene, medical, system safety, product assurance, research or development, and administration. The product safety function is usually a staff rather than a line position, although it may include duties of both.

Responsibilities

The responsibilities of the product safety professional may include some or all of the following:

- Develops policies and procedures

- Secures and analyzes data from all operating divisions, including, but not limited to, product safety hazard analysis, loss trends, warranty or guarantee claims, product incidents and claim history, production volume, sales volume, distribution and use data as needed to accurately define the extent of possible future liability

- Reviews quality assurance, control, and safety procedures, specifications, test records, and sampling plans to ensure that existing quality and safety standards are met

- Submits periodic progress reports

- Studies new developments, new procedures, or changes in procedures and systems

- Develops communications systems

- Develops and assists in implementing training for all production, sales, customer relations, customer service, and other personnel, stressing knowledge of the required product safety features and how to communicate them to the user

- Develops a recording system for product accidents, field failures, and customer accidents

- Coordinates claim handling

- Coordinates loss investigations

- Follows up on preservation of evidence

- Maintains liaison with business, professional, governmental, and standards organizations to keep current on codes, standards, regulations, industry accepted practices, labeling, and use of outside testing

- Represents the company on committees and assists other company officials on committees

- Acts as chairperson or secretary of the product safety committee

- Reviews recall procedures and crisis communication plans

Company Policy and Management Support

Although not all manufacturers have issued product safety policy statements or procedures manuals, those who have normally include a statement concerning product safety efforts. A policy statement demonstrates management's interest and effort in producing safe products. In developing such a statement, organizations may find it helpful to review examples developed by other companies.

PROGRAM ORGANIZATION

No consensus exists about the best way to organize a company for product safety, as no two companies operate in exactly the same way. Even though many different organizational structures have been developed, there is no clear favorite in either large or small companies. As a result, the product safety program is formalized in some companies, but not in others. Many companies find it helpful to create product safety committees to manage their safety programs.

Product Safety Committee

Product safety committees generally coordinate safety efforts within a company. They are especially useful when a company launches a new product safety campaign within its organization. Almost one half of all larger companies have established one or more product safety committees at various corporate levels and locations to supplement or reinforce the work of full-time or part-time product safety professionals. Within most companies that have such a committee, it reports to the highest level of general management. The group's primary role is to recommend policies, provide advice to top management, and audit product safety performance. Committee makeup will vary according to the business organization. For example, key committee members from a manufacturing company will almost always represent the following departments:

- Product design or engineering

- Manufacturing

- Purchasing

- Quality assurance

- Service, marketing, or installation

- Legal

  In the case of a retail firm, buyers and sales departments would be represented on the committee.

  In addition, sales, advertising, insurance, personnel, public relations, health, safety, environmental affairs, and purchasing department representatives should be designated and be prepared to serve as consultants to the product safety committee when such expertise is required.

  The duties of the product safety committee may include:

- To establish guidelines and review all printed matter (advertising, product brochures and labels, direction and instruction sheets, and maintenance guides) for clarity and conformity to laws and regulations of all federal, state, and local acts and codes—including National Highway Traffic Safety Administration, Food and Drug Administration, Consumer Product Safety Commission, Occupational Safety and Health Administration, Department of Transportation, Federal Trade Commission, Department of Agriculture, and the Treasury Department.

- To establish guidelines and criteria for the identification and evaluation of product safety hazards and their associated risks that might result in personal injury, illness, property damage, or product performance deficiencies caused by transport, installation, use (or reasonably foreseeable misuse), maintenance, service, repair, or disposal of new products, their placement, or the upgrade of existing products.

- To establish basic procedures for the design, development, and testing of effective instructions and warning labels, to be used with all products having significant risks that cannot be eliminated by product design changes or that could result from reasonably foreseeable misuse.

- To have legal counsel review all product warranties, guarantees, exculpatory clauses, disclaimers, and liability release statements and warnings.

- To supervise the preparation and issuance of any written notification to an international, federal, state, or local regulatory agency regarding a product defect or noncompliance with safety standards, codes, or regulations.

- To develop written procedures for product recall, notification of the public, and corrective steps.

In conclusion, regardless of the structure of the product safety department's organization, it will have a great deal in common with other functions or departments, as well as some significant differences. However, the keys to the department's success are related far more to the degree of top management support than they are to the organizational structure a company has selected for its product safety function.

EMPLOYEE INVOLVEMENT

Obviously, many segments of the organization and, thus, many people are involved in activities that can impact product safety. To further the efforts of management and the product safety program, all employees must become aware of ways they can improve product safety. It is neither possible nor desirable for the product safety professional to train or educate all persons in the safety-related aspects of their work. Instead, the professional should use existing job-training systems, with input from the training coordinator. In the case of overall product safety orientation and awareness training, however, the coordinator should be directly involved in planning programs, workshops, and other materials. Employees should communicate to the product safety professional any manufacturing or user comments related to product safety issues. Again, normal practices for training should be employed in order to put safety on equal footing with other personnel and operations matters in which all organization members are trained. One priority of the product safety professional who works in a design or engineering-oriented company would be to augment the product safety awareness and knowledge of the designers. Because of their engineering education, most designers are aware of certain basic safety concepts, such as redundancy, guarding, safety devices, failure modes, and safety factors. However, they may not be aware of specific system safety techniques, such as failure mode and effect analysis, operations, hazard analysis, or fault tree analysis. Many companies conduct safety awareness programs to further guarantee that all aspects of safety are adequately considered during the design engineering phase. The checklists in Tables 2–1a through 2–1d are used by some companies to assist designers and to promote product safety awareness.

Text continues on page 31.

Table 2–1a.   Checklist of Design Concepts

☐ KISS (Keep It Simple Stupid)

☐ Fail safe

☐ Positive lockouts

☐ Emergency shutoffs

☐ Prevention of inadvertent actuation

☐ Prevention of unauthorized actuation

☐ Shielding and guarding

☐ Proper material for operation

☐ Accessibility of adjustment and servicing locations

☐ Failures in design

☐ Foreign material sensing and elimination

☐ Prevention of modification

☐ Isolation of operator from point of operation

☐ Consider human factors in design of controls

☐ Provide proper safety equipment

☐ Provide overload and overspeed warnings

☐ Training programs

☐ High-feasible factor of safety

☐ Redundant systems

☐ Proper components selected

Table 2–1b. General Checklist of Design-Related Hazards

☐ Weight

☐ Flammability

☐ Speed: high or low

☐ Temperature

☐ Toxicity

☐ Sharp edges

☐ Rotating parts

☐ Reciprocating parts

☐ Shrapnel, flying objects

☐ Stability, mounting

☐ Visibility

☐ Pinch and crush points

☐ Noise

☐ Light: strobe effect, intensity

☐ Radiation

☐ Chemical burns

☐ Sudden actions

☐ Height

☐ Heat

☐ Cold

☐ Pressure, vacuum

☐ Emissions

☐ Explosions, implosions

☐ Vibrations

☐ High frequency and radio waves

☐ Slick finishes

☐ Surface finish

☐ Flames and sparks

☐ Electrical shock

Table 2–1c. New Equipment Checklist

Product

☐ Are adequate guards and shields provided for moving parts, such as chains, sprockets, cutters, fans?

☐ Are there preventative arrangements to stop operation of the product or warn the operator when the guards or shields are removed (interlocks)?

☐ Are there any unprotected sharp edges on components of the product that could harm the user?

☐ Are there any built-in provisions to limit operation of the product to within safe conditions, (e.g., speed control, dead-man control, electrical ground, fuses, safety valves)?

☐ Is the unit grounded?

☐ Are there any provisions to prevent the operation or use of the product by unauthorized persons?

☐ Are permanent safety warning notices affixed to the product to alert untrained users regarding potential hazards?

☐ Is the product safe when left unattended? If not, are there any measures taken to make the product safe when unattended?

☐ Are there any redundancies in critical areas of the product to secure safety operation (in brakes, mechanical lock design, electrical interlock)?

☐ Is rated capacity indicated on the product by means of an attached plate, stamping, cast legend, or other permanent means?

☐ Has consideration been given to potential secondary use accidents during the expected life of the product?

☐ Are sales and service personnel well informed and aware of limitations and safe use of the product?

☐ Are there chemical or vapor hazards?

☐ Have noise levels been checked?

Operator's/Owner's Manual

☐ Is there an operator's/owner's manual and/or a training video?

☐ Are advice and/or warnings given concerning any inherent hazards? Are safety and operational hints provided?

☐ If installation is to be made or assembly performed by the purchaser, does the manual stress safe methods and practices?

☐ Is the manual clear and understandable?

☐ Are the important installation and assembly operations sufficiently stressed by underlinings, bold print, and so on for safe and proper installation and assembly?

☐ Are safety instructions summarized in the front of the manual as well as given throughout the manual?

Table 2–1d.   Machine Safety Critique

Project No.   _____

Client Name   _____

Project Leader   _____

1. What powers the machine?

    a. Air   _____
                psi

    b. Hydraulic   _____
                     psi

    c. Electric   _____
                  volts

    d. Other   _____

    Comment: _____

2. Is there a catastrophic hazard that could harm any nearby persons or the surrounding environment?

    a. Fire?   ☐ Yes   ☐ No

    b. Explosion?   ☐ Yes   ☐ No

    c. Mechanical failure?   ☐ Yes   ☐ No

    d. Electrical failure?   ☐ Yes   ☐ No

    e. Chemical or high pressure release?   ☐ Yes   ☐ No

    f. Other?   _____

    Comment: _____

3. Are there unguarded entanglement or pinch points on the machine?

    a. Nip or pinch points (pull rolls, feed rolls, infeed or removal mechanism, chains and sprocket, gears, V-belts, or other)?   ☐ Yes   ☐ No

    b. Smooth rotating shafts?   ☐ Yes   ☐ No

    c. Protrusion on rotating shaft or other moving part?   ☐ Yes   ☐ No

    d. Other   _____

    Comment: _____

Table 2–1d.   Machine Safety Critique continued

4. Are there electrical hazards?

    a. Ungrounded electrical circuit, without ground detector lights?   ☐ Yes   ☐ No

    b. Grounded control circuit, without permanent ground?   ☐ Yes   ☐ No

    c. Is any portion of the machine not grounded?   ☐ Yes   ☐ No

    d. Is static electricity a hazard?   ☐ Yes   ☐ No

    e. Other   _____

    Comment: _____

5. Is there a possibility of operator contact or exposure to the following hazards?

    a. Hot or cold surfaces or material?   ☐ Yes   ☐ No

    b. Chemically harmful material?   ☐ Yes   ☐ No

    c. Intense light (arc welding, spot welding)?   ☐ Yes   ☐ No

    d. High-pressure fluid or gas (leaking air, oil, steam, other)?   ☐ Yes   ☐ No

    e. High-level noise?   ☐ Yes   ☐ No

    f. Other possible "contacted by" exposure   _____

    Comment: _____

6. Are there latent hazards?

    a. Are there any "delayed action" hazards due to unreleased pressure, kinetic (coasting) energy, batteries, electrical capacitance, potential (falling) energy or other causes?   ☐ Yes   ☐ No

    b. Are there any machine elements turning at high speed which could be unseen or appear stationary due to work lights and stroboscopic effects?   ☐ Yes   ☐ No

    c. Will accumulation of scrap material represent a fire, jam, or cleanup hazard?   ☐ Yes   ☐ No

    Comment: _____

Table 2–1d.   **Machine Safety Critique** continued

7. Are there pollution hazards (fumes, sprays, fine particles, heat, odor, smoke, allergenic, or other)?　　☐ Yes　☐ No

Comment: _____

8. Are there nonmoving hazards (sharp corners, edges on machine)?　　☐ Yes　☐ No

Comment: _____

9. Is the machine properly assembled (no loose bolts, incomplete wiring, loose or leaking fluid lines)?　　☐ Yes　☐ No

Comment: _____

10. Are there mechanical failure hazards?

   a. Do the machine elements appear strong enough?　　☐ Yes　☐ No

   b. Have strength calculations of critical areas of concern been made?　　☐ Yes　☐ No

Comment: _____

11. Are there maintenance hazards?

   a. Does the machine have to be operating while being lubricated, adjusted, or cleaned out?　　☐ Yes　☐ No

   b. Are the guards placed over frequent (everyday) maintenance points hinged with lockout switches?　　☐ Yes　☐ No

   c. Does the machine have a single lockout function that shuts the machine down completely and can be controlled by the maintenance person (i.e., by padlock)?　　☐ Yes　☐ No

   d. When electrical power is released, is all air or hydraulic pressure also released?　　☐ Yes　☐ No

   e. Do maintenance point guards have appropriate warning signs on them?　　☐ Yes　☐ No

Comment: _____

12. Are there operator hazards?

   a. Is it possible to remove jam-ups without hazard after all power to the machine is off (no latent spring force, pneumatic or hydraulic pressure, sudden restart)?　　☐ Yes　☐ No

---

Table 2–1d. **Machine Safety Critique** continued

    b. Are there emergency stop controls within easy reach of normal working, maintenance, repair, and adjustment areas of the machine?   ☐ Yes   ☐ No

    c. Will a sudden reflex action of the operator (as to clear a jam) expose him or her to hazard?   ☐ Yes   ☐ No

    d. Are permanent work platforms, stairways, handholds, footings, handrails, and slip-resistant surfaces included where necessary?   ☐ Yes   ☐ No

Comment: _____

13. Are warnings adequate?

    a. Are precautionary instructions permanently affixed to the equipment? Examples: "For use with 110-volt electrical supply only." "Do not adjust, clean, or repair unless the power is shut off." "Replace shields before operation."   ☐ Yes   ☐ No

    b. Has an Operator's Manual and/or video, with instructions regarding the proper adjustment, operation, and maintenance of the machine, been provided?   ☐ Yes   ☐ No

Comment: _____

14. Are safety controls adequate?

    a. Is there a means of locking out the START function with a STOP function in close proximity to the machine?   ☐ Yes   ☐ No

    b. Does the handle on the electrical input power box disconnect all power when it is opened? Can it be locked in the disconnect phase?   ☐ Yes   ☐ No

    c. If any automatic control system element malfunctions or a power failure occurs, will it cause hazard to the operator (high-temperature cut-off, improper application of normally opened or normally closed valve, incomplete electrical or mechanical interlocking of functions)?   ☐ Yes   ☐ No

    d. Are all operating controls color coded, if necessary, and provided with a clear word description of their function?   ☐ Yes   ☐ No

Comment: _____

Table 2–1d.   **Machine Safety Critique** continued

15. Are there potential hazards in transferring the machine to the customer?

    a. Will the machine be placed on a skid or have suitable lifting or attachment points for loading and transportation to and installation at the user's location?   ☐ Yes   ☐ No

    b. Are there special installation or machine use instructions that should be given to the customer?   ☐ Yes   ☐ No

    Comment: _____

16. How many hours or cycles has the machine been operated in our shop?

    Comment: _____

17. Have OSHA requirements, state and local code requirements, and special client-designated standards been reviewed and does the machine comply?   ☐ Yes   ☐ No

    Comment: _____

    Pictures are to be taken of the machine with all guards and warning signs in place and included in the permanent file of the Machine Safety Critique.

    Project Leader: _____

    Date: _____

    Safety Committee Representatives: _____

    _____

    _____

    Date: _____

    Shop Representative: _____

    Date: _____

Product safety professionals working in companies that do not design the products they sell may conduct safety awareness training for other personnel, such as buyers of retail establishments. They may find the following successful training methods useful:

- Using case studies

- Providing a safety library

- Conducting safety seminars for engineers, production workers, field service workers, and others

- Sending personnel to outside courses and seminars on ergonomics, system safety analysis, product liability law, and other safety-related subjects

- Sending representatives to the field to see how the products are used, so they gain a fuller appreciation of how people use the products

- Distributing compiled accident statistics to engineering staff and involved personnel

- Sponsoring qualified personnel to participate in voluntary safety-related organizations, such as the National Safety Council, the American National Standards Institute (ANSI), the National Fire Protection Association (NFPA), the American Society of Safety Engineers (ASSE), the American Society for Quality Control (ASQC), and the American Society for Testing and Materials (ASTM), and others

Specialized Job Training

The product safety professional may be asked to propose or supervise safety-related job-training programs and to recommend or purchase ready-to-use materials. To develop a new program and/or review an existing one, the coordinator should know the steps in developing a successful training program and the basic principles of learning.

Program Development
Development of a successful program may be broken down into the following six steps:

- *Determine the Training Needs*
This may be done through systematic analysis of the existing and potential problems and their solutions; through an analysis of the required knowledge and skills of each job; through job observation, knowledge or performance tests, interviews, and written questionnaires.

- *Set Training Objectives*
  These should be clear statements of the desired outcomes. The objectives should tell what the employees must learn and how the trainer will know they have learned it.

- *Select Methods, Media, and Materials that Meet Objectives*

- *Obtain and/or Develop Training Program*

- *Conduct Program*
  Apply the principles of learning, of testing to determine how well educational objectives are met, and of reinforcing learning through rewards. Consider issuing a company diploma to those who complete the program. It will demonstrate the company's commitment, motivate continued employee attention to product safety issues, and facilitate periodic review of qualifications.

- *Evaluate Program*
  Assess the reactions to the program through anonymous questionnaires. Measure the knowledge gained, the skills developed, and the resulting effects upon the company.

Principles of Learning

Employee trainers must know and be able to apply the five basic principles of learning: readiness, association, involvement, repetition, and reinforcement.

Readiness

Readiness refers to the learner's emotional state and motivation. An individual must *want* to learn before he or she is *ready* to learn. The trainer can help create that desire to learn by letting the learner know how important the training is, why it should be learned, and the benefits to be gained. These benefits include professional growth, recognition, making the work easier and safer, giving the worker more challenge and variety, and increasing the worker's potential.

Association

Association of the known with the unknown makes it easier to learn new material. The trainer must start with known tasks or ideas and build in simple steps to the new and more difficult tasks and ideas. Using comparisons, contrasts, and examples helps workers form associations from the known to the unknown material.

Involvement

Involvement in the learning process is essential for understanding and retention. The trainer should involve as many of the learner's five senses as possible. The trainer can have the worker use hands-on practice, do repetition drills, engage in question-and-answer sessions or group discussions, use audiovisual aids, discuss case problems, do role playing or simulations, take quizzes, and do application exercises.

Repetition

Repetition aids learning, retention, and recall. The trainer should stress accuracy before speed to avoid the learner's having to unlearn a bad habit.

Reinforcement

Reinforcement should always accentuate the positive. The learner should experience successes and receive praise, rewards, and recognition. The trainer should make the positive feedback timely and specific.

The trainer, whether someone inside or outside the company, should know the job to be taught, know how adults learn, thoroughly prepare the material to be taught, and be patient. The trainer can ensure the success of the program in the following ways:

- Help the learner build motivation by helping him or her set goals.

- Show interest in the learner.

- Provide learning and performance incentives.

- Be a good role model.

- Use positive reinforcement.

- Expect and be patient with uneven learning rates, individual differences, learning spurts, and forgetting.

- Do follow-up in unobtrusive, nonjudgmental ways.

In assessing and/or developing a training program, the product safety professional should ensure that the above principles are followed by all trainers involved in the program.

3

Product Design and Evaluation

In many cases, products involved in accidents are judged as unsafe or unreasonably dangerous even though the product functioned as designed and did not malfunction. It is not enough for a product merely to fulfill its intended function reliably; other design characteristics can lead to accidents. As a result, the actual design of a product is probably the most important criterion by which product safety is judged. A major concern of product safety professionals must be to ensure that design review and/or other measures are followed in every design project.

Designers must always consider safety as of primary importance in designing a new product or revising an established one. To incorporate safety properly into product design, it should be given comparable priority to function and cost, and should not be subservient to any of the many commercial concerns, such as aesthetics, manufacturability, etc.

Designers also must be aware of developments in related industries as well as unrelated industries. The latest developments in other fields of engineering, chemistry, medicine, psychiatry, environment, and ergonomics can affect the safety of a product's design.

Obviously, it is economically desirable to make provisions for safety while the product is in the early conceptual stage to avoid having to redesign significant portions of the product to accommodate later safety provisions. In fact, there is no substitute for designing an acceptable level of safety into the product before the product is piloted for manufacture.

DETERMINING PRODUCT REQUIREMENTS

Seldom are new products so novel that they are created totally "from scratch," that is, without any significant reference to existing or older products. Broad requirements of all kinds, including safety, often can be established based on the knowledge of preceding designs.

Design safety requirements for radically new products frequently can be quite explicit regarding cost, function (performance), and other specifications. However, they seldom can be as explicit when it comes to setting target levels of safety—except, of course, for drugs and other products for human consumption or contact and except when a particular safety feature, specification, or safety attribute is among the initial design requirements.

As initial safety requirements are likely to be broad or incomplete, designers typically must rely on some implicit or derived safety goals. These goals are "derived" in the sense that they are neither explicitly stated nor apparent from the functional requirements of the product. Derived goals are necessary partially because sufficient data of accident/injury rates for various design alternatives do not exist for most products. Even when substantial data are available, few established criteria exist to distinguish acceptable from unacceptable accident frequency and severity rates. Furthermore, at the earliest stages of a design project, it might be impossible to make any but the broadest and most general assessments of the item's safety or reliability level. Better assessments can be made when some of the functional requirements have been engineered into "harder," physical specifications.

PRODUCT SAFETY ENGINEERING

Most of the basic concepts, source materials, and methods used in product safety engineering have come from the more general discipline of safety engineering, which developed during the occupational safety movement that began early in this century. Two basic concepts have gained special prominence in the fields of product safety and occupational safety. The first concept is the safety engineering hierarchy of priorities:

1. Eliminate hazards.

2. When hazards cannot be eliminated, provide feasible safeguards against them.

3. Provide warnings and personal protective equipment against the remaining hazards.

The second basic concept is the accident prevention program triad, the three E's of accident prevention. To prevent accidents, it is necessary to:

1. Remove hazards through engineering whenever feasible;

2. Educate (train) people to perform tasks safely; and

3. Enforce safe behaviors through effective management controls.

These general concepts of safety cannot be applied to product safety as thoroughly as in other situations. It is not always possible to remove hazards in products through engineering. A product provider or manufacturer has little if any control over how a product may be adapted to fit into a system involving a group of products, nor over the ancillary equipment and personal protective equipment that will be used. Moreover, the product designer has, at most, only partial control over the environment and circumstances of use, especially in the case of consumer products. Although the manufacturer can provide instructions and warnings on or with the product, these efforts do not constitute an acceptable education program, judged by industrial safety criteria. Finally, virtually no enforcement measures can be incorporated into products because product users are typically not supervised and not under the scope of relevant laws or regulations.

Therefore, designers must be especially careful about the elements of a product that are under their control. The "eliminate-guard-warn" rule may be useful in a workplace in which hazards are often unique and temporary, but the rule offers little specific guidance to product designers. For instance, it does not specify which functionally caused hazards are unacceptable, which means of safeguarding are desirable in particular situations, what sacrifice in utility can be tolerated in safeguarding a hazard, exactly how to present warnings, which kinds of warnings are necessary, how significant a hazard must be to require a warning, and an endless number of other, more detailed questions likely to surface at almost any stage of a design project.

Whether to eliminate, guard, or warn is not a question designers can consider and answer only once during product development. Instead, safety questions need to be considered repeatedly as the design project progresses from concept to detailed requirements. At each stage, designers must design in safety, using all the guidelines the profession has to offer. System safety engineering and ergonomics techniques, described later, can be applied to advantage.

REFINING PRODUCT REQUIREMENTS

The designers may have various interpretations of the safety requirements. As the work progresses, it is possible and necessary to make the requirements more explicit.

Two major tasks of product safety professionals are to ensure that product safety requirements are (1) set at the start of the project and (2) refined at all stages of the project. The latter point is particularly important, because it is difficult to write detailed safety requirements until other product elements have been established. For example, some aspects of ergonomics may be impossible to address until a prototype is made.

The process of refining product requirements (which is not limited to safety requirements) lies at the heart of managing design engineers (Figure 3–1). If management controls the work of individual design engineers too tightly, especially at early stages, it stifles creativity and decreases technical novelty. On the other hand, when management controls are too loose, the product may fail to meet critical time, budget, and other commercial requirements. Besides the use of day-to-day informal and formal management practices, most organizations (especially large ones) use a series of design reviewers to further refine product requirements. (There is a difference between controlling and reviewing. For instance, detailed design must be intensively reviewed but must not be so tightly controlled that designers are prevented from exploring all the options.)

A third major task for product safety professionals is to ensure that design personnel have enough knowledge about safety engineering and accident prevention to make professional safety judgments and decisions. Product safety professionals should ensure that designers know the following for each of the goals or courses of action in Table 3–1:

- When/how/which safety issues should be raised for each of these goals
- Safety results of each of these goals
- Legal ramifications of each of these goals

The implicit design safety requirements used by individual designers at the earliest stages of a new product are derived from one or more of the following goals or courses of behavior listed in the Table 3–1. (The safety requirements are ordered from "most objective" and "most mandatory" to "most subjective" and "most optional" to meet or exceed safety requirements.)

Figure 3–1.
A product safety professional reviews product designs with an engineer using a computer.

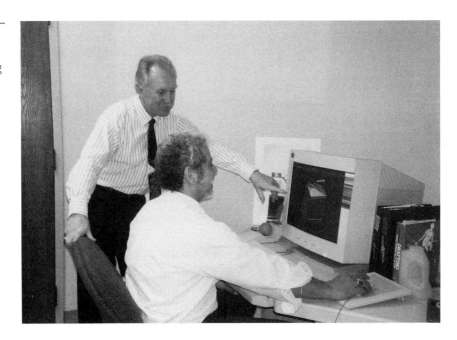

Table 3–1.   Designer's Prioritized Product Safety Mission

- Design against safety-related functional aberrations.

- Conform to any laws or government regulations.

- Design to meet the requirements of the certification authorities.

- Comply with industry and consensus standards.

- Conform to industry practice (what is used in recent similar products and what customers/users expect).

- Achieve or advance the state of the art (employ technologies as advanced as or more advanced than those used in other recent similar products).

- Use best professional judgment, including review by other professionals.

DESIGNERS' SAFETY GOALS

Design against Safety-Related Functional Aberrations

The following are brief overviews of the three areas of knowledge designers need regarding each of the major goals listed in Table 3–1.

Common law demands that products perform the function they are designed and intended to perform without failures and aberrations that would injure the user or others. The term "product integrity" is used to describe this concept. For example, chairs must not collapse under the weight of a person, machinery must not speed up when a stop button is pushed, and a hammer must not splinter when striking an ordinary nail. Such failures violate any of several tenets of the common law as well as the meaning of good product engineering.

This not to say that products must never fail. In fact, virtually all products eventually fail. It is the mode of failure that is important. A bicycle wheel could get a flat tire or become bent, but it must not suddenly disengage from the bicycle because users do not guard against this occurrence. Such a failure can cause serious injury. Neither should it be inferred from common law that safety-related failures must never occur. Users are expected to exercise due care when using products, monitoring and maintaining them to prevent safety-related failures or aberrations caused by wear and tear, aging, damage, or abuse. Manufacturers must provide users with proper maintenance and operating instructions for the product life cycle. However, the bicycle owner, to use the example above, is expected to have a faulty axle repaired before the wheel fails on the road.

Designers naturally seek to create a product that functions reliably, and this desire is entirely consistent with achieving acceptable safety. The ability to successfully execute this desire depends mainly on engineering competence.

Designers should consider three ways to meet the first derived safety requirement: (1) provide extra reliability for components or attributes that could likely cause injury upon failing; (2) provide for inherent warning signals, such as the squeaking of overworn brakes, to warn users that the product needs attention; and/or (3) extend the expected life of safety-related components or attributes.

Conform to Laws or Government Regulations

The design of some products sold in the United States, such as children's toys, is partially or entirely controlled by governmental regulations and laws. Compliance is mandatory. For example, the Consumer Product Safety Act provides regulations for the design of children's toys, some fabrics, and other consumer products. Some consumer products containing chemicals are regulated by the Hazardous Substances Control Act. Some major safety aspects of motor vehicle design are mandated by the National Highway Traffic Safety Administration. The Federal Department of Transportation oversees packaging and labels for hazardous substances. Food, food packaging materials, and drugs are regulated by the Food and Drug Administration (FDA). Other particular products are regulated by the Department of Agriculture and other agencies.

Such governmental regulation may go beyond the design itself and cover additional activities such as design testing and manufacturing quality control. A major example is military equipment contracted by the Department of Defense. Such contracts state not only the end-product specifications, but also the way in which much of the design work is to be contracted.

Although most product design is not regulated, the body of federal regulations of products is nevertheless huge and is beyond the scope of this publication. However, some important generalizations about government-contracted design activity can be made. For example, companies must maintain close communication with the appropriate regulating agency or agencies to avoid misinterpreting the regulations. Companies may misinterpret not only the aspects of the product covered by the regulations, but also the legal requirements themselves. Many organizations employ specialists to collect and disseminate regulatory information.

Certain benefits counteract the difficulties of dealing with governmental regulations. Generally, regulations preempt some of the engineering/design judgments. The law recognizes this by allowing a legal presumption that a product that complies with the relevant regulations is not defective. However, courts have not always upheld this presumption, particularly when the regulations themselves were found to have been so poorly conceived or worded that the designer or manufacturer should have recognized an existing problem that resulted in an accident. More detailed discussion of the legal aspects of government regulations is beyond the scope of this publication.

CE Mark

The European Union (EU) has issued a set of health and safety directives that consumer and industrial products must meet in order to be sold in the EU. Products that conform to the directives and their associated standards are identified with the CE mark, Conformité Européenne.

Currently, there is a short list of product categories for which the CE mark is mandatory for an item to be sold in the EU. In 1994, toys became the first group of products the EU registered in this way. Telecommunications terminal equipment and simple pressure vessels used in manufacturing followed. As of January 1, 1995, machinery and personal protective equipment was required to have the CE mark to be sold in the EU. (See *The Machinery Safety Directive*, 89/392/EEC).

In the next five years, however, the number of affected products that will need the CE mark is expected to increase dramatically to include medical devices, child-safety articles, marine equipment, and low-voltage items, such as toasters and refrigerators. Eventually, roughly 50%, or $50 billion worth, of U.S. exports to Europe will need the CE mark, according to the U.S. Department of Commerce. (Graham, 1995)

There is a growing awareness among industries that the EU product safety requirements and CE mark will become world standards. This is evident as more countries participate in the International Organization for Standardization (ISO) 9000 and 14000 initiatives on quality and environmental management systems. See Table 3–2 for a list of relevant standards and dates they became effective.

Design to Meet Requirements of Certification Authorities

It has become customary in many industries to submit certain products to an independent testing organization such as Underwriters Laboratories, Inc.; Factory Mutual; or the American Gas Association prior to marketing the product. Examples of such products include certain types of personal protective equipment, fire extinguishers, and many electrical components and appliances. The testing organizations evaluate the product design against a standard sponsored by the laboratory or by another standards-writing organization. Some product certifications issued by standards organizations also involve monitoring manufacturing and quality control activities by having staff members conduct facility inspections and product sample testing.

Table 3–2.   Status of EC Directives*

Short Title of Directive (Number)	Date CE Marking Can Be Used	Date CE Marking Is Mandatory
General Product Safety (92/59/EEC)	June 1992	—
Low Voltage (73/23EEC)	Jan. 1995	Jan. 1997
EMC (89/336/EEC)	Jan. 1992	Jan. 1996
Machinery (89/392/EEC)	Jan. 1993	Jan. 1995
Safety Components (under 89/392/EEC)	—	—
Medical Devices (93/42/EEC)	Jan. 1995	June 1998
Active Implants (90/385/EEC)	Jan. 1993	Jan. 1995
Simple Pressure Vessels (87/404/EEC)	July 1990	July 1992
Toys (88/378/EEC)	—	Jan. 1990
Telecom (91/263/EEC)	July 1989	July 1992
Gas Appliances (90/396/EEC)	Jan. 1992	Jan. 1996

*All directives are amended by Directive 93/68/EEC

When it is customary to have a product approved by an independent laboratory, the company has no option but to conform to the laboratory's standard. Such products often must be certified or listed by the laboratory in order to be marketed successfully in the United States or certain other countries. When certification is not customary, but a recognized laboratory has issued a standard, the decision to comply with this standard should be guided by the manufacturer's criteria for using industry and consensus standards.

Comply with Industry and Consensus Standards

The two goals discussed above are options for only a small fraction of design engineers. Much more frequently, designers deal with products largely unregulated by the government and not subject to any kind of independent laboratory approval. As a result, the most concrete design guidelines for most products are voluntary industry and consensus standards.

The distinction between industry standards and consensus standards is the degree of participation among various segments of society in writing each type of standard. Industry standards are written by professional societies, testing laboratories, industry and trade groups, and other professional organizations. Any of these groups can initiate or sponsor a standard. However, it cannot become a national consensus standard unless a wide range of interested parties are represented and there is a procedure for public debate to ensure that a consensus truly exists regarding the standard's contents.

In the United States, the American National Standards Institute (ANSI) is a group that oversees the consensus-gathering procedure. These national consensus standards bear an ANSI designation and identifying number.

Although such standards are voluntary, a company's decision to comply is very important. One of the first things the product safety professional must do is become aware of all industry safety standards and national consensus standards applicable to the company's products. Besides the consensus standards published and coordinated by ANSI, other important sources of product standards include Underwriters Laboratories, Inc. (UL); Society of Automotive Engineers (SAE); American

Society for Testing and Materials (ASTM); National Electrical Manufacturer's Association (NEMA); National Fire Protection Association (NFPA), National Printing Equipment and Supply Association (NPES); American Society of Mechanical Engineers (ASME); American Society for Quality Control (ASQC); International Organization for Standardization (ISO); and other voluntary organizations. Write to ANSI and to these organizations for the catalog of standards (see Appendix 6, References). Safety professionals should check with the appropriate experts within their companies to gain information about applicable product safety standards.

The most important standards for products sold internationally, especially in the European Union, are those issued by the ISO. The ISO published the 9000 Series of Quality Management and Quality Assurance Standards in 1987. Roughly 25,000 manufacturing sites in Europe and North America have received ISO 9000 registration since that time. The ISO 9004, *Guidelines for Quality Management and Quality System Elements*, first edition, 3/15/87, recommends that a company should identify the safety aspects of products or service quality with the aim of enhancing product safety and minimizing product liability. Steps should be taken both to limit the risk of product liability and to minimize the number of cases by:

a) identifying relevant safety standards in order to make the formulation of product or service specifications more effective;

b) carrying out design evaluation tests and prototype (or model) testing for safety and documenting the test results;

c) analyzing instructions and warnings to the user, maintenance manuals and labeling and promotional material in order to minimize misinterpretation;

d) developing a means of traceability to facilitate product recall if features are discovered compromising safety and to allow a planned investigation of products or services suspected of having unsafe features.

Regarding traceability, Section 16.1.3 recommends the following identification system:

> The marking and labelling of materials should be legible, durable and in accordance with the specifications. Identification should remain intact from the time of initial receipt to delivery to the final destination. Marking should be adequate to identify a particular product in the event that a recall or special inspection becomes necessary.

Section 15.4 recommends investigating possible causes of product quality problems:

> The relationship of cause and effect should be determined, with all potential causes considered. Important variables affecting the capability of the process to meet required standards should be identified.

The product safety professional must also consider broad voluntary standards that apply to products on the basis of construction characteristics rather than by the specific name. Principal examples are products incorporating gears, chains, and other mechanical power transmission apparatus and products with electrical, ventilation, pressurized, heating, or laser components. Safety standards do exist for products that include such components.

Relatively few national standards are safety standards. Most are issued mainly to promote standardization of products and services of different origins. Compliance with nonsafety standards is, in general, a purely commercial decision without legal or safety considerations. The safety professional should determine, however, whether the nonsafety standards, indeed, have no safety ramifications.

Although compliance with consensus safety standards is voluntary, decisions to use designs that do not comply with such standards must be studied thoroughly by more than one individual in a company. Any noncomplying designs should be proved to be as safe as or safer than the standard design. Also, the rationale behind a decision to use a nonstandard design must be well documented. This is because the existence of the standard creates a presumption, in effect, that the standard design is the preferred, safer one.

On the other hand, the decision *to use* a standard design should be made with almost as much care as a decision *not to use* it. Design engineers must consider whether the applicable product standards truly provide for a reasonably safe product in light of what they know of industry practices and the state of the art. Complying with consensus safety standards has, on occasion, been judged not to provide sufficient safety for users. (If there are no applicable consensus standards in certain situations, it is advisable to consider initiating either a company internal standard, industry standard, or ANSI standard for the specific type of product.)

Conform to Industry Practice

Regardless of whether applicable standards exist, design engineers must consider the safety aspects of industry practices. Industry practice refers to the ways in which tasks are generally performed and to the type and features of tools, equipment, and machines used by members in an industry to complete those tasks. Design engineers have at least two sets of industry practices to consider—the practices of their own industry (e.g., widget producers) and those of their customers (e.g., widget users). Although producers' design practices may suggest some of the users' practices, designers must make concerted efforts to learn user's practices. If the designer's products are sold to more than one industry, there may be additional relevant sets of practices that apply to the products.

Manufacturers try to make products consistent with industry practice to sell the product and to increase the safety for users. Making products that deviate from long-established standards or conventions can cause users to make errors, resulting in accidents. For example, to design a machine with a START button in the position conventional practice has designated as the STOP position may cause users to make mistakes that lead to accidents. Human factors experts have listed many recommended conventional practices based upon psychological responses, such as the direction of machine movement that users anticipate when they manipulate a control knob.

The law generally allows industry practice to be considered as a factor in support of (or against) the merits of a particular design. As a result, conforming to industry practice generally poses no dilemma to designers trying to produce a safe product. This fact is fortunate because industry practices can be deeply ingrained and highly resistant to change from any source, including equipment suppliers.

However, companies also can be faced with difficult decisions about whether to comply with industry practices. These decisions can arise when industry practice is found to be unsafe, as evidenced by past accident experience, or when industry practice becomes contrary to established consensus safety standards. Companies can resolve these difficulties by using the following approaches:

1. Design products that discourage the unsafe practice or make it less risky.

2. Change or initiate an industry standard with regard to the unsafe practice.

3. Change the applicable laws or regulations.

For example, operators of certain types of packaging machinery routinely attempted to fix jams without first stopping the equipment (an unsafe industry practice). Producers of such machines responded to this hazard by increasing the use of jam sensors to automatically stop jammed machines and by providing additional barriers to prevent users from reaching into moving machine parts. Eventually, this issue was resolved by a more stringent ANSI standard.

The equivalent of industry practice also exists for consumer products. For example, it became apparent that many users of an acid drain cleaner were not reading and following the directions for its proper, safe use. Although there were no alternative products that were as effective for all situations, the producers removed such cleaners from the market in favor of alkaline drain cleaners which required fewer special instructions for safe use.

Not all unsafe user practices, however, can be addressed through product modifications. Sometimes the only practical preventive measure is to attempt to change the unsafe procedure. For example, during the preceding decades, despite the fact that virtually all electrically powered industrial equipment was powered through safety switches with a lockout feature, unexpected start-up of machinery while repairs were underway resulted in many deaths and amputations. Over the years an increasing number of industry standards have added a section on locking out equipment under repair or have begun to reference and adopt the ANSI Z244 and 29 CFR 1910.147 lockout/tagout standards. If there are no consensus standards for an industry that has an unsafe industry practice, it is advisable to consider initiating either an industry or ANSI safety standard. Another approach is to submit papers about the unsafe practice to industry or trade magazines, alerting others to the hazard.

The above sample approaches are practical and logical solutions. However, if no practical or feasible alternatives exist to eliminate or modify known unsafe practices, the individual design engineer needs to warn product users through signs and instructions. (Warnings are discussed in Chapter 4, Product Communications Design.) If there is no industry practice with regard to a new product feature, there is, in effect, an *implied default industry practice. Namely, a new product feature should be no less safe than the feature in existing products that will be replaced by the new product feature.*

Achieve or Advance the State of the Art

State of the art refers to a level of technology that can be achieved without the need for new scientific research and with commercially available components and materials. To be state of the art, a product must use the latest commercialized level of technology (e.g., computerized controls versus discrete transistors, vacuum tubes, relays) and demonstrate the latest operating functions as measured by the important parameters (such as speed, output, safety, quality, uptime, waste, accuracy, versatility) which are relevant to the products' usage.

Suppliers who fail to provide state-of-the-art products are likely to lose their customers and may even go out of business. Competition tends to push product manufacturers and industrial users alike to adopt state-of-the-art technology. Similar pressures push consumers to demand and consumer product manufacturers to supply state-of-the-art products.

Using the latest state-of-the-art technology, however, is not necessarily synonymous with maximizing safety. Often there are problems associated with adopting leading-edge technology. For example, in some heavy industrial environments the simplicity and established reliability of relay circuitry makes it the technology of choice despite the availability of newer technologies. Thus, the state of the art is not homogeneous, but varies from industry to industry and, sometimes, from product to product.

Even though lagging behind the state of the art often poses a greater sales problem than a safety problem, there are situations when conforming to the state of the art is critical to safety. Both product safety professionals and designers should analyze technical developments and their application to their particular industry to determine if they face any of the following situations:

- New technology may eliminate a hazard. For example, automatic spooling devices on some film processing machinery eliminated the mechanical hazards associated with manual spooling.

- New technology may eliminate tasks associated with accidents. For example, some operators of a particular machine oiled components while they moved. An automatic, central oiling system eliminates the need to do this task in an unsafe way.

- New technology may enhance reliability of a safety-critical assembly. For example, new electronic sensors can signal control systems of impending aberrant mechanical motion.

- New technology may be "inherently" safer. Low-voltage control systems and a noncombustible degreasing agent are examples.

- New technology may make a formerly unusable safety device or feature feasible. Examples include magnetic position sensors to provide the capability to interlock guards located in hazardous environments and the advent of reliable "easy start" engines for lawn mowers which make it more practical to put a "dead man switch" on mower handles.

There is no broad legal requirement mandating companies to adopt the latest technology in the design of new products. Design engineers should use the following criteria when making such decisions:

> When new technology provides a feasible alternative and the alternative design is significantly safer in terms of expected accident frequency and/or severity, the existence of the alternative design, if not used, can result in the existing design being deemed unreasonably dangerous, if it is found to have caused an accident.

Use Best Professional Judgment

The first six derived goals cited in this section usually provide an excellent foundation for safe design and usually serve as good benchmarks for evaluating the safety of designs. However, when there are no standards, regulations, or industry practices, safety benchmarks also do not exist. Nevertheless, companies are still under the obligation to design a product free of unreasonable risks, meaning that companies must employ other means of evaluating the safety of each proposed design. In these situations, designers often must rely on their own best professional judgment.

Reliance on professional judgment is most critical (1) when evaluating new design alternatives, (2) when the alternatives appear to provide uncertain or inconsistent levels of safety, and (3) when one or more product functions are adversely affected by proposed safety features. Such decisions have both engineering and legal ramifications.

Making professional judgments is more subjective than the six other product safety goals. To create the greatest confidence in these design decisions, companies should seek the opinions of other professionals who understand the use of the product and its accident potentials as well as the science, mathematics, and techniques of the related engineering fields. Three areas in particular help designers develop safe products and deserve special attention:

- System safety
- Ergonomics/human factors
- Predicting foreseeable misuse

These topics are covered in the next three sections of this chapter. For further discussion of foreseeable misuse, see Chapter 10, Risk Management.

SYSTEM SAFETY— OVERVIEW

System safety engineering, a technique developed in the aerospace industry, approaches safety engineering based on the concept that a system must be treated in a holistic manner. The concept therefore includes techniques that consider the mutual effects of interrelated elements of the system on one another throughout the system's life cycle. When adapted to product safety programs, system safety engineering can help to focus safety efforts on the product as it is used in a particular environment throughout all phases of its life cycle. Such an approach is especially helpful to manufacturers trying to overcome problems associated with controlling consumer use of their products.

System safety analysis is accomplished by the use of various logic diagrams along with qualitative and/or quantitative data on component failure. The results of such an analysis can reveal design, operating, and other factors that can improve system reliability and quality, as well as safety. In *System Safety Analysis Handbook* (July 1993), the System Safety Society discusses 90 different system safety hazard identification and evaluation techniques.

A full-scale system safety analysis may require specialists with access to sophisticated computer equipment and software. However, basic forms of these techniques, such as MORT (Management Oversight and Risk Tree), Fault Tree Analysis, and FMEA (Failure Mode and Effect Analysis) require only paper and pencil and an individual trained in one of the techniques. Informal use of these techniques can help individuals focus their thinking regarding product or system safety and reveal undesired system conditions that otherwise might go unrecognized.

SYSTEM SAFETY— METHODS

The *Military Standard for System Safety Program Requirements*, MIL–STD–882B, defines system safety as "The application of engineering and management principles, criteria, and techniques to optimize safety within the constraints of operational effectiveness, time, and cost throughout all phases of the system life cycle." The following are some of the distinctive characteristics of the system safety concept:

- The "system" is considered *as a whole*—a combination of interacting, interrelated, or interdependent elements, including hardware, software, personnel, procedures, and facilities, functioning within the operational environment.

- System safety requires an organized, orderly, *systematic* approach to achieve maximum safety.

- The primary objective of system safety is to identify and control hazards *before* mishaps can occur. Engineering and management principles, criteria, and techniques are employed to that end.

- Safety efforts are applied throughout the *life cycle* of the system, from conceptual planning through disposal of the system elements.

Although originally developed and applied in the aerospace industry, system safety principles have been used for a broad variety of transportation, utility, industrial, and consumer products as well. Some advantages of this approach for product safety programs are:

- The product is considered in the context of how and where it is used rather than in isolation. This approach encourages designers and others to consider product interactions with other elements of the "system(s)" in which the product may be used, including persons who will use it, service it, or otherwise be affected by it.

- A thorough, orderly, systematic approach increases the chances of meeting product safety goals.

- The preventive nature of the system safety approach helps to identify product safety requirements without relying on accident experience as a basis. This characteristic is especially valuable when the product has not been used or has been in use only a short time.

- Attention to safety needs in all phases of a product's life cycle is appropriate, as different requirements may exist or become evident at different stages of product development, production, use, service, and disposal.

The system safety discipline includes a number of safety analysis methods for identifying system hazards "before the fact." These techniques can be divided into two broad categories, as follows:

- Deductive logic methods, which reason from the general to the specific. The Fault Tree is an example of this type of analysis. It begins with a speculated undesired result and identifies the events and combinations of events that could cause that result. A diagram is constructed, tying the events together through logic gates that show their relationships. Such an analysis can be quantified if probabilities are known for all the lowest level events. Even without quantifications, a Fault Tree Analysis provides valuable insight into the interaction of potential causative events—providing a sort of "roadmap" of critical paths.

- Inductive logic methods, which proceed from the specific to the general. Failure Mode and Effect Analysis is an example of this kind of approach. Designers and others list the components of the product and analyze each failure mode to identify its effect on the system. The technique can be applied to functional elements as well. This type of analysis is especially useful to appraise the effects of failures in components or system elements.

The thought processes involved in these analytical approaches can be applied even if the formal, structured techniques are inappropriate. Checklists of hazards in specific product applications, many of which can be found in the literature, are helpful aids in safety analysis. (See Tables 2–1a through 2–1d in Chapter 2 for sample checklists.)

Other system safety principles that have broad usefulness are found in MIL–STD–882B. Among them are "System Safety Program Objectives," "System Safety Design Requirements," "System Safety Precedence," and "Risk Assessment." For example, "System Safety Precedence" specifies "the order of precedence for satisfying system safety requirements and resolving identified hazards." The order is as follows:

- Remove the hazard through design.

- Reduce the risks to an acceptable level by incorporating the prescribed safety devices.

- Provide proper warning devices.

- Develop procedures and training.

System safety principles will be most valuable in product safety programs if tailored to the particular application rather than *"forcefit"* for all applications.

ERGONOMICS/HUMAN FACTORS

Ergonomics, or human factors, is the study of how humans relate physically and psychologically to machines and other physical objects in their environment. It includes a study of both human capabilities and limitations. The goal is to use this knowledge to design jobs, workplaces, and products that will be safer, more comfortable, and more efficient for workers.

This field includes the study of anthropometrics (or the size of human body parts), human strength, speed, agility, perceptions, habits, cognition, and other mental or psychological attributes. When ergonomics is not adequately considered, product users are at greater risk for injuries from overuse or overexertion. Too many repetitions of the same part of the body or repetitive motions involving too much force can increase the incidence of pain or injury in various susceptible parts of the body, such as wrists and lower back. These injuries have become major causes for lost time due to accidents in industry in recent years.

Product designers must be aware not only of these human physical capabilities and limitations but also of certain human behavioral tendencies. For example, some people tend to make mistakes while under stress or in a hurry. Others routinely use products in ways for which they were not designed. Unfortunately, studies also show that some people are not very good at assessing hazards while others pay little attention to warnings, as indicated by studies of those who resist or ignore warnings of floods, tornados, or tidal waves.

In addition, product designs that involve transmitting performance data back to users, such as computerized machine tools, must take into account the format and layout of the data. Otherwise, people may not understand the current status of the product and make mistakes. The process of avoiding such user mistakes through product design is called "situation awareness assessment."

The manufacturer has a duty to make a product that is safe under normal use and under reasonably foreseeable misuse or to warn consumers about substantial hazards that may result from normal use and reasonably foreseeable misuse. Designers of products that involve repetitive or forceful body motions can refer to the NIOSH *Equation for the Design and Evaluation of Manual Lifting Tasks* for definitions of "repetitive" or "forceful." Machine designers can refer to ANSI B11.TR 1-1993, *Ergonomic Guidelines for the Design, Installation, and Use of Machine Tools*.

Consideration of human factors and system safety analysis are specifically required in many research contracts issued by the government. These analyses can be done in-house or can be contracted to outside consultants. The product safety professional should evaluate how these techniques are used among technical staff and encourage their use, whenever practical.

PREDICTING FORESEEABLE MISUSE

In the past, consumers who misused a product were barred from successfully pressing a claim for injury against the manufacturer, seller, or others who were involved in providing the product. In recent years, some courts have departed from this precedent and now allow such claims, if the misuse was reasonably foreseeable and if the consequences of such misuse were not obvious.

Therefore, product designers must now consider the "reasonably foreseeable misuses" of their products. In the process of determining reasonably foreseeable misuse, designers also face the concept of "unreasonable misuse."

An example may help to clarify what is a reasonably foreseeable misuse. It is known that standing on the top cap and highest step of a stepladder is not safe, yet it is also known many people will do so despite the risk. Therefore, many ladder manufacturers issue a warning advising users not to stand on the top cap and the highest step to caution them against this reasonably foreseeable misuse.

It is also conceivable that someone would use a stepladder as a roof jack, leading perhaps to the collapse of the ladder and the roof. Most courts would probably not judge such use of a stepladder reasonable, so this could be deemed unreasonable misuse instead of reasonably foreseeable misuse. Signs warning against unreasonable misuses are not necessary, even though most misuses, such as using a ladder as a roof jack, can be imagined.

Evaluating whether a misuse is reasonable or unreasonable could be a subjective decision. However, one reason for accumulating field use data, claims experience, and ergonomics test data is to try to gain an objective basis for anticipating misuse. The product safety professional should determine whether the following three guidelines are among those considered in the company's efforts to uncover possible misuses:

- Are there environments other than the anticipated environment in which the product could be used? (e.g., Could a product intended to be used indoors be used outdoors?)

- Are there likely alternative ways of using the product for the intended purpose? (e.g., Could a front loading shear be fed from the rear?)

- Are there likely secondary uses of a product that could result in unintended usage and hazards? (e.g., Could a paint sprayer be used to spray cleaning solution?).

Once the product safety professional has uncovered misuses, he or she must determine whether they are reasonably foreseeable. This task is an important reason why the product safety professional should ensure that comments from marketing or market research are obtained during the design process and during the product safety review process. Such data can help the safety professional draw composites of typical user characteristics such as age, sex, size, education, and training and identify the environmental factors that may contribute to produce misuse.

Also, it is important to learn from customers about all the uses they have in mind for the product. Some companies have included product safety items on market research studies. Some firms even determine possible harmful misuse by having products tested by a laboratory that employs selected users. Product safety professionals often visit industrial facilities that use their company's products to observe and interview actual users. They also encourage design engineers to do the same. These field visits and observations can be part of a company's formal new-product safety review procedure. The safety professional can make certain such activities are adopted or other means are available for designers to gain knowledge of product use and misuse.

DESIGNING SAFETY REVIEWS AND CERTIFICATION

At predetermined points in the design process, the design should be checked for compliance with its requirements. The objective of this process is to ensure that the optimum product design is achieved. This process is called the design review or product certification procedure. Although it can be formal or informal, establishing a formal procedure can be an advantage for the company in the event of product liability litigation.

For many years, most larger companies have done formal engineering reviews of all newly developed products. Formal safety design reviews are not the same as straight design reviews—the safety review group may include nontechnical as well as technical specialists. The focus of the group is safety rather than the many technical and commercial concerns that arise in the design process.

Self-Certification of Products

Self-Certification by Producer or Supplier, ANSI Z34.2–1987, prescribes general procedures for certifying products in-house. Some companies use these procedures for certifying the safety of their products. Other companies have organized their own internal safety approval procedures—often involving teams, review committees, or task forces who develop their own safety criteria and evaluate new products against such criteria. Even when safety criteria in the form of standards or regulations exist, many companies choose to judge designs against their own (often more stringent) criteria as well. Many self-certification procedures include reviews of ancillary items, such as instruction books, manuals, packaging, servicing, spare parts, and so on. When this is the case, representatives from the affected work groups are included in the review group.

Formal Safety Design Review

The formal design review is a scheduled systematic review and evaluation of the product design by a team that includes personnel who are not directly associated with the product's development. However, all members of the team, as a group, *are* knowledgeable in and have a responsibility for all elements of the product throughout its life cycle, including design, manufacture, packaging, transportation, installation, use, maintenance, and final disposal. The review group must include people familiar with how, when, and where the product is used so that all possible uses and reasonably foreseeable misuses are considered.

Some organizations do not perform a product safety design review separate from their regular review. In this case, the company must make special efforts to give sufficient attention to the safety of the product. Some companies, particularly consumer product manufacturers, invite impartial outsiders to sit on a product safety review panel. Companies with product safety professionals usually have them sit on review committees, sometimes as chairpersons.

Besides designers and engineers, reviews for product safety often include quality specialists (to ensure that provisions for adequate quality control are incorporated into the design) and production personnel (to ensure that the production capabilities—both physical and human—are not mismatched with the design requirements).

Obviously, there are many ways to conduct product safety design reviews. The product safety professional must make certain the method chosen (1) gives product safety considerations sufficient attention; (2) provides an element of impartiality toward the design in the product safety design review group; (3) ensures that the best knowledge of the design is included in the product safety review; and (4) provides for follow-up on assigned actions to ensure their completion.

Companies selling products manufactured by outside vendors can employ a similar review procedure for new products before they are merchandised. An effective review process should include the following elements:

- Review the intended use of the product.

- Investigate foreseeable reasonable product misuse.

- Initiate product safety hazard analysis.

- Assess the risks associated with potential safety hazards.

- Review tests to quantify the safety-critical features.

- Determine the cause of product safety hazards.

- Eliminate the cause by re-design.

- Review safety certification and regulatory approvals.

- Verify that the product can be manufactured to specification.

- Review warnings where design changes are unfeasible.

- Supply instruction manuals and training for operators.

- Conduct alpha (in-house) and beta (customer) testing.

- Review advertising, promotional, packaging materials.

- Establish file for calculations, safety decisions, and tests.

- Follow and document product changes after introduction.

- Conduct additional reviews for product changes.

CONTROLLING DESIGN CHANGES

The product safety professional should check the procedures established for making design changes that have an impact on safety. Design changes should be made (1) to correct an outright mistake and (2) to improve a product design, which can include reducing cost. At many companies product improvement changes take place continuously. A single major industrial product might undergo hundreds or even thousands of changes in the course of a few years. A recent study concluded that a typical design engineer performs 50 design changes per year—almost one per week. When design changes are made under these circumstances, errors can occur which would not always be fully documented. Some of those errors could affect product safety.

To reduce the risk of product safety-related design mistakes, procedures for process control should include the following items:

- All design changes must be approved by designated management.

- All reasons for and details of a change must be documented.

- If possible, design changes related to product safety should be made so that improvements can be adapted to existing designs.

- Design changes related to product safety should include evaluation of the need to recall existing products or to contact current users.

- No product design changes should be permitted in the "field" or in the manufacturing plant unless approved and properly documented.

- If appropriate, a special review system should be established for changes related to product safety.

Design and engineering are increasingly being done on computers instead of on paper. Design change procedures are generally built into computer-aided design (CAD) software. CAD users should ensure that their system enables them to follow the above procedures.

AGING AND DISCONTINUED PRODUCTS

Product safety professionals should also be concerned about the existence of aging and discontinued products (products probably in use but no longer being manufactured). Unlike the development of new products or updated product lines, often the product safety professional has little opportunity to use existing product safety design review structures and procedures to help determine how safe are the designs of these aging or discontinued products.

In this situation, the product safety professional can use four methods to identify potential accident or injury risks:

1. Gather historical experience data about the product.

2. Interview individuals who are the most knowledgeable about the details of these designs.

3. If possible, visit places where these products are used to identify potential accident situations.

4. Track and evaluate sales of replacement parts to determine design-related problems.

When products are discontinued, it becomes impossible to implement some standard accident prevention measures. However, a company might be able to initiate other injury prevention programs, such as recalls, retrofits, and safety bulletins.

SAFE DISPOSAL OF PRODUCTS

Ongoing market research indicates that consumers are increasingly aware of and concerned about how products affect the environment. Because of this new awareness, manufacturers worldwide now routinely consider environmental impact issues along with product safety. Therefore, the safety professional should evaluate the company's product disposal methods along with issues of foreseeable consumer safety and property damage. A product design review should consider the environmental effects of the product and its disposal on humans and on the land, water, and air.

The following are typical questions that may be asked when reviewing product designs for environmentally safe disposal:

• Is there an opportunity to eliminate an environmental problem through the design process?

• Do options exist for minimizing or eliminating waste after products are discarded by consumers?

• Has a chemical safety hazard review been conducted to identify any flammable, corrosive, reactive, or toxic waste materials or by-products?

• Does the product use an environmentally sensitive substance (e.g., PVCs or CFCs)? Have less toxic or hazardous substitutes been explored?

- Has a search been conducted to identify banned substances in the U.S. and international markets?

- Is there a way to increase the product's life cycle?

- Has everything been done to decrease the types and amounts of component materials?

- Has the product been designed for safe disassembly?

- Has the product been designed so that as many components as possible can be reused?

- Have all packages and inserts been reduced or eliminated wherever possible?

- Have materials been chosen to fit into an identifiable waste stream for safe recycling and/or disposal?

There are many state, federal, and international laws and directives and subsequent court decisions that are relevant to the safety, health, and environmental effects of products. A manufacturer that has questions about the health and environmental effects of an existing or new product should conduct scientific testing that will address any concerns. All testing should be verified and documented.

REFERENCES

Dorris AL and JL Purswell. "Human Factors in the Design of Effective Product Warnings." *Proceedings of the Human Factors Society— 22nd Annual Meeting*, 1978.

Graham S. "Europe puts its mark on U.S. product safety." *Safety & Health Magazine*, Jan. 1995, pp. 32–33.

Liker JK and WM Hanrock. "Organizational Systems Barriers to Engineering Effectiveness." *IEEE Transactions on Engineering Management*, Vol. EM–33, No. 2, May, 1986, pp. 82–91.

Roland HE and Moriarty B. *System Safety Engineering and Management*, 2nd ed. New York: John Wiley and Sons, 1990.

Safety System Society. *Safety System Analysis Handbook*. Albuquerque, NM: NM Chapter, System Safety Society, July 1993.

Third-Party Certification Program, ANSI Z34.1–1982. ANSI, 11 West 42nd Street, New York: NY 10036.

4 Product Communications Design

Product communications, in a product safety context, include manuals, advertising, assembly instructions, warnings, signs, stickers, pictures, and so on. Such written communications are of great concern to the product safety professional because they are considered as part of the product. Any item that is part of the product (e.g., warnings, instructions) should have a part number so it can be reordered by users. This is especially important for long-lived products, such as machine tools.

Although written materials can present potential liability problems, they also provide an opportunity for training and communications. Such materials are typically the company's only means of ongoing communications about the product to the user. Many manufacturers use the first section of their manuals as a product safety section, summarizing the warnings highlighted elsewhere in the product manual and printed or placed on the product (Figure 4–1a and 1b).

CRITERIA FOR WHEN TO WARN

Product safety warnings should be used only after all possible hazards have been eliminated through the design process. Designers need to understand, first, that current research seems to indicate that warnings, in general, and reminder messages, in particular, have limited effect in changing user behavior. Thus, designers should not have any great confidence in the ability of safety messages to prevent unsafe practices. This realization also might prevent designers from relying on these messages to achieve desired safety results when a feasible safer design alternative is available. Second, designers need to understand that it is mandatory that they provide the prescribed warning messages giving information needed to ensure user safety. Third, they must know the requirements that any acceptable warning must meet.

Figure 4–1a.
This sample Owner's/Operator's Manual discusses safety information for an injection blowmolding machine. Note that it is ready to be packed and shipped to the user.

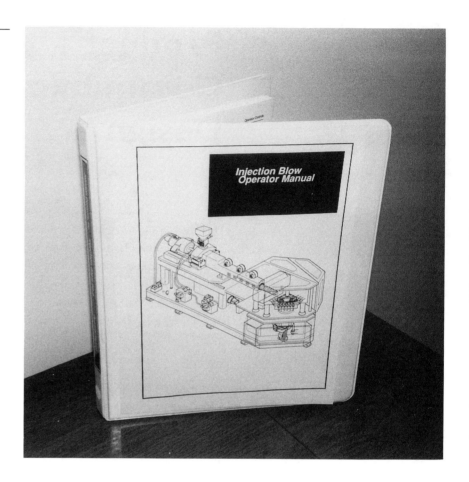

Figure 4–1b.

Safety instructions and warnings are provided in the first chapter of the Owner's/Operator's Manual. This sample shows the first page only.

1.1 Safety

All reasonable precautions were taken to assure the safety of personnel using your new injection blow molding machine. The operator must be trained and practice safe operating procedures at all times on and around the machine. Warning, Mandatory and Prohibition signs are placed to alert personnel to hazards and precautions to use.

 All of our machine lines must be operated with the prescribed safety devices (guards, inter-locks, signs) properly positioned and in good working order, as originally designed and installed. The absence of these safety devices from an IBM machine line which appears in any of our manuals, training programs or sales media occurs solely for display purposes.

1.2 Safety Precautions

- Do not operate machine unless safety gates and interlocks function properly.

- Ensure that all fixed guards are intact and secured. Repair or replace any damaged guards.

- Wear safety glasses, particularly around equipment used for trimming or grinding.

- Protect yourself from skin contact with hot plastic. Molten or freshly molded plastic, orheated machine parts can cause serious burns. Wear proper personal protective equipment. Shoes with soft soles help prevent slipping on spilled pellets and oil.

- Clean up spilled oil and pellets immediately.

- Be certain all safety devices are working properly.

- Before starting any equipment and during equipment operation be certain all sprockets, chains, belts, and pulleys are covered.

- Avoid "cold" start-ups, which could damage equipment.

- Turn off and lock out main power to the machine before working on electrical equipment.

- Turn off and lock out main power to the machine when adjusting or performing maintenance procedures.

- Turn off hydraulic pump, and release and lock out air disconnect before working between molds or mold halves.

- Do not climb on equipment and gauges while machine is in operation.

- Inspect all heat instruments and other gauges for proper control.

- Insure all service functions (air, water, electric) are properly installed and operating.

- Check tightness of tie rod nuts.

- Check all hydraulic pressure lines and fittings. Loose joints or piping could result in an oil blow-out.

- Check electrical grounding.

- Check all electrical wiring for loose connections or potential short circuits.

- Use approved ladders and approved portableladder stands when necessary to service machine.

 Request from your resin supplier a Material Safety Data Sheet (MSDS) to determine which, if any, health hazards are present during the plasticizing process.

The duty to warn users of product dangers and to instruct them in safe use of the product is an expanding theory of product liability law. In such cases, the plaintiff's attorney does not attempt to prove that the product itself is defective or unreasonably dangerous, but rather that the safety messages or instructions were inadequate, thus rendering the product, as a whole, defective. Lawsuits against products typically incorporate an allegation of insufficient or improper warnings regardless of whether warnings were provided. Such an allegation often serves as a backup in the event that the plaintiff is unable to establish defect in product design or manufacture. As a result, *when* to warn and *how* to warn are both important questions for companies. In general, the following criteria should be observed.

A manufacturer must warn or instruct when:

- The product has significant injury potential, that is, has significant risk of injury

- The manufacturer knows or should have known of the risk of injury

- The expected or typical user is unaware of the danger and does not normally guard against it

These criteria regarding when to warn the user include the following ideas:

- Unintended product uses and misuses are not necessarily excluded; there remains a duty to warn users of dangers resulting from reasonably foreseeable but unintended use or reasonable and foreseeable misuse of the product. (See Chapter 3, Product Design and Evaluation, for a discussion of "reasonable" and "foreseeable" behavior.)

- A duty exists to warn the user of dangers resulting from using the product in foreseeable, hostile environments (i.e., excess heat or cold, moisture, and so on).

- There is no duty nor is it desirable to list all the things for which the product should *not* be used. Trying to do so inevitably would result in an incomplete list that could be used to imply that all unlisted uses are safe. To minimize this possibility, labels should deal only with foreseeable, reasonable misuses and uses, as discussed above.

- No warning is necessary in situations where the product presents an open and obvious danger and the actions to avoid the danger are also obvious. For example, hand-tool makers do not have to warn users to avoid placing a hand in the path of a saw or under a hammer. However, in many instances what is obvious to a designer may not be obvious to an average user. The manufacturer should consider the experience and knowledge of the user when designing safety messages.

- No warning is necessary where the dangers are commonly known to the public or to the relevant trade or profession. For example, warnings such as "Do not drive automobiles over open fields" or "Do not attempt to drive regular nails in concrete" are not necessary.

- Some products have inherent hazards that are open and obvious but for which safety measures are *not* all obvious. Warnings must be provided, but they only need to cover the measures that are not obvious. For example, it is necessary to warn of the suffocation risk of burning charcoal indoors, but it is unnecessary to warn against picking up a hot briquette with one's bare hand.

- It is relatively rare, but occasionally the manufacturer has a duty to warn the user against making foreseeable product changes or modifications which would tend to make the product more dangerous. For example, the company should warn users of some multipurpose machinery to replace or alter the original safety features when the original safety devices are not appropriate to other expected uses.

- The manufacturer may have a duty to warn even a small fraction of users of a potential sensitivity or allergic reaction when the danger is not commonly known. Usually, laws and government regulations describe whatever warnings are necessary for such agents.

- Not all hidden hazards carry a duty to warn. By their nature, some products cause users to guard against certain hazards. For example, pots and pans and other kitchen implements do not require a warning about their possibly causing a burn. Plastic products that can emit toxic by-products when burned do not need to carry a label warning users not to burn them in the living room fireplace.

COMMUNICATION REQUIREMENTS

The product safety professional, with the aid of engineering or other departments, if necessary, should review all product communications and make sure that the safety messages they contain fulfill the following three requirements:

• Warnings must clearly describe the possible consequences, especially personal injury, of not heeding the warning, particularly when the consequences are not obvious.

• When safety procedures are not obvious, warnings must clearly inform the user what to do or what not to do to avoid injury.

• Warnings must identify all hazards that are not obvious.

The above requirements are derived from common law, which recognizes that sometimes the hazardous consequences or safety procedures are obvious and do not have to be expressed. For example "CAUTION: HOT SURFACE" and "DANGER: 480 VOLTS" are acceptable warnings.

Two additional requirements apply to safety signs that appear on the product itself:

• The sign or label must be located on the product so the warning is conspicuous.

• The sign or label must be constructed so it is visible and lasts for the intended life of the product.

PRODUCT SAFETY PROFESSIONAL'S ROLE

The product safety professional should review all communications to be sure they are written in the appropriate language(s). Symbols should also be used where appropriate. Local regulations may require various types of special warnings on certain products.

Writing effective warnings for all except the simplest products usually requires a collaboration between a knowledgeable technical writer and the designers and engineers or scientists who are most familiar with the product.

Those responsible for product safety usually have the following roles to play:

1. Review the content and wording of the message(s) to make sure it conforms to the applicable requirements above.

2. Review the content and format of warnings. There are mandatory regulations covering the format of safety signs used in the workplace (OSHA) and covering the format and content of certain consumer product decals (Hazardous Substances Act and Consumer Product Safety Act). For most unregulated products, the voluntary standard ANSI Z535.4–1991 should be followed. See the section on Safety Sign Specifications later in this chapter.

- Assure that designers and engineers recognize when a warning is needed so that one is provided.

- Review the placement of safety messages on the product to ensure that they are conspicuous and properly sequenced. Sequencing means locating the warning so that it is encountered before the user has an opportunity to encounter the hazard that is the subject of the warning. For remotely controlled devices, warnings should be duplicated at the control panel.

- Review advertising and sales literature to make certain that only safe usage messages are conveyed and that product performance and suitability statements are not exaggerated or misleading.

Naturally, companies should ensure that all safety communications are as easy as possible for the intended user to understand. However, writing clear materials for specific audiences is a special skill that companies should assign carefully to the proper personnel.

PLACEMENT OF WARNINGS

Sometimes it is not possible to put warnings directly on the product because of environmental reasons or space limitations. If the warning requires a long explanation or some time to understand completely, or if it must be presented as part of a long series of operating instructions, it should be placed in the owner's/operator's manual rather than on the product itself (Figure 4–1a). In general, users are more likely to take time to read a manual than a label on a product. A brief warning notation on the product should refer the user to the owner's/operator's manual.

WARNINGS VERSUS INSTRUCTIONS

There is a perceived difference between *warnings* and *instructions* or *directions*. In general, instructions or directions are designed to promote effective use of the product; but in this context, informing users about any dangers is secondary. Warnings, on the other hand, emphasize potential hazards or dangers and specify the proper actions the product user must take. In general, the courts have tended to find that insufficient warning is the same as no warning in terms of fulfilling the duty to warn. Therefore, manuals accompanying products have begun not only to give clear and easily interpreted instructions on how to use the product, but also to provide clear and specific warnings of any inherent dangers or possible misuses that could result in injury—similar to the purpose that safety signs on products themselves are meant to serve.

Accepted practice has been to include warnings into owner's/operator's manual so that the user reads the information along with the instructions. To make warnings distinct from the instructions, companies should use standard formats, colors, or symbols to highlight any safety-related warnings (Figure 4–1b). In this manner, warnings contained within manuals will reiterate safety signs or stickers on the products. Third-party certifiers and government regulations may specify the language and placement of warnings within the manual.

Properly formatted instructions should include:

- A summary safety section at the front of each manual

- Safety symbols or typography that distinguishes injury warnings from other instructions/directions

- Photographs, drawings, or other illustrations meant to supplement written instructions

- Information pointing out typical reasonably foreseeable misuses

- Notice of special installation tools and procedures

- Reproduction of warnings placed on the product

- A parts list that includes product numbers for safety signs and decals so they can be reordered

- Details about where and when lockout procedures are necessary

- Parallels between safety signs and information on the product and in owner's/operator's manual

- Advice to the typical product user about when specific tasks should be delegated to someone with special qualifications and skills or to the product manufacturer, particularly in regard to consumer and industrial products

Because of space limitations and the lengthy instructions needed for specialized machinery or other complex products, it is impractical or impossible to place complete operating instructions on the product—even when the instructions include critical safety information. Many manufacturers choose to place a decal on the product that briefly describes its operation, but refers users to a specific section in the owner's/operator's manual for *full* details. In many companies, the first section of manuals is used as a product safety section that summarizes the warnings highlighted elsewhere in the manual and on the product.

Rather than placing detailed installation, operation, and maintenance guidelines within one manual, many manufacturers issue separate manuals for each topic area. Obviously, this means that workers will not have to read or try to understand sections that are not relevant to their jobs.

Warning labels for chemical products also require special care. The Toxic Substance Control Act and "Right to Know" laws describe how to write a label for unregulated as well as for regulated chemical products.

SAFETY SIGN SPECIFICATIONS

The American National Standards Institute (ANSI) consensus standard for designing product safety signs applicable to consumer and industrial products is ANSI Z535.1, .3, and .4—1991. There are five parts to this standard: Z535.1, *Safety Color Code*; Z535.2, *Environmental and Facility Safety Signs*; Z535.3, *Criteria for Safety Symbols*; Z535.4, *Product Safety Signs and Labels*; and Z535.5, *Accident Prevention Tags*. This standard provides information regarding the proper signal words, formats, colors, symbols, letter sizes, and so on. For products directed to the international market, several International Organization for Standardization (ISO) and International Electrotechnical Commission (IEC) standards should be reviewed, including ISO 3864 (1984). Safety signs for chemical products have been standardized per specification in ANSI Z129.1— 1988, *Precautionary Labeling of Hazardous Industrial Chemicals*. ANSI standards continue to be referenced by OSHA and applied accordingly. Certain products may need warnings that are product-specific and required by laws or regulations.

The product safety sign layout specified by ANSI Z535 is shown in Figure 4–2a. The upper panel is used to display one of the signal words: DANGER, WARNING, CAUTION. The lower panel is for the message. The optional panel (left side) is to show a recognizable symbol or pictogram. Although the ANSI Z535 standard indicates that the symbol or pictogram is optional, best practice dictates that one of these should be used whenever possible to reinforce communication of the hazard. Designers of warnings must realize that in the event of litigation, the plaintiff's legal team is likely to suggest "better" ways that the warning could have been communicated.

Some manufacturers are currently providing bilingual product safety signs on their machines. The format is illustrated by the signs in Figures 4–2b and 4–3a (English and Spanish).

Figure 4–2a.
This is the general format for product safety signs. Source: American National Standard Institute standard Z535.4–1991.

OPTIONAL

SYMBOL
OR
PICTOGRAM

SIGNAL WORD

MESSAGE

Figure 4–2b.
The ANSI Z535 standard requires that the signs shall have rounded or blunt corners, be free from sharp projections, and be located so as not to produce a hazard. The message should be easy to understand and contain sufficient information to respond properly. ANSI Z535.4 indicates an optional graphics panel for display of a pictogram or symbol to supplement the message panel. This reflects the need to communicate as effectively as possible with those who do not read the English language. This sample product saftey sign illustrates ANSI Z535.4 requirements.

The ANSI Z535 standard requires, in addition, that the signs shall have rounded or blunt corners, be free from sharp projections, and be located so as not to produce a hazard. The message should be easy to understand and contain sufficient information to respond properly (Figure 4–2b).

Safety sign specifications that apply to European Union products include the following:

- 89/392/EEC; Machinery Safety Directive, Annix 1, Section 1.7.2, Warning of Residual Risks

- prEN 500 99–1; Indicating, Marking, and Actuating Principles. Part 1—Visual, Audible, and Tactile Signals

- IS 3864; Safety Colours and Safety Signs (Figure 4–3b shows an example of an ISO safety sign.)

PICTOGRAMS

ANSI Z535.4 indicates an optional graphics panel for display of a pictogram or symbol to supplement the message panel (Figure 4–2a and 2b). This reflects the need to communicate as effectively as possible with those who do not read the English language. When expected users may be illiterate or speak a language other than English, a graphics panel should be used where possible and effective. (See graphic signs in Figures 4–2b and 4–3a and b.)

Graphics messages, however, are appropriate only for the simplest messages, such as "Wear Goggles," or "Electrocution Hazard." Even for simple messages, there is a risk that readers will misinterpret the meaning of the symbol or pictogram. Some misrepresentations called "critical confusions" impair the reader's ability to understand a message. ANSI Z535 provides criteria for testing messages for critical confusion.

Figure 4–3a.
This is an example of an ANSI safety sign.

Figure 4–3b.
This is an example of an ISO safety sign.

For this reason ANSI Z535.4 refers to yet another standard, ANSI Z535.3, which shows illustrations of acceptable graphics to communicate particular hazards. If it is foreseeable that a particular safety sign will need to be understood by people who do not read English, one of the symbols or pictograms in Z535.3 should be incorporated in a separate panel of the sign (Figure 4–2b).

When dealing with a hazard or hazard consequence message that is not covered by the standard, a new graphic will need to be created if the sign is to contain a graphics panel. In this event, ANSI Z535.3 requires that the graphic be tested with intended viewers before publishing and using the sign. The Z535.3 standard contains guidelines for conducting such testing and criteria to use to judge the acceptability of test results.

Without an in-house artist or other source of expertise, it can be difficult to prepare the various panels of a new sign for printing. Fortunately, companies that print signs often offer layout, color specification, typesetting, and graphics services as part of the printing job. They can also advise a company on materials specifications, including adhesives. In addition, software is available to help companies comply with standards, including pictograms. When relying on these services, the buyer should ascertain the vendor's familiarity or expertise with the relevant ANSI and/or other applicable standards.

EFFECTIVENESS OF INSTRUCTIONAL METHODS

Providing educational videotapes is an excellent idea, especially for a complex product. Videotapes have become the method of choice for training workers. It is important for companies to realize that the illiteracy rate in the United States is now about 25%. Using video presentations can help companies communicate their training messages to workers with poor reading and comprehension skills. When using video presentations, management should consider these points:

- Show only the proper, safe use of the product.

- Review all warnings and cautions that apply to the product.

- Present the product accurately, without exaggeration.

- List the product's limitations and hazards of misuse.

- Before duplicating and distributing the videotape, have the finished video and script reviewed by the appropriate legal and technical staff, including safety professionals.

It is presumed in common law that persons exposed to safety signs should read and follow the warnings and that failure to do so by someone injured in an accident (in the absence of extenuating circumstances) can be regarded as negligence on the part of the product user. Concurrently, it has become better known that failure to provide adequate product warnings can cause the product manufacturer to be held responsible for an injury. These two legal doctrines together with the increased frequency of claims against products have helped create a viewpoint that more warnings are preferable to fewer warnings. In turn, this has fueled an increase of safety signs on new products, especially industrial products.

For example, in the early 1970s, it was possible to tour a machine shop without finding a single safety sign on any of the machinery. Today, by contrast, it is virtually impossible to find any new machine tool without one or more warnings. This is the case even for the simplest machines, such as drills and bench grinders. The increase in safety signs has occurred during a period when the need for them seemed to be decreasing because companies were building more and better safeguarding features into many products.

Design engineers observing this trend may conclude that safety signs have been increasingly acknowledged to be effective accident preventers, and they may decide to join the trend and use more of them. Yet many or most of the additional product warnings are not warnings in the traditional sense; instead, they are reminders to use safe practices or to refrain from unsafe practices. (Bogget & Rodriguez, 1987) "Traditional" warnings such as DANGER: PRESSURIZED STEAM and CAUTION: COMBUSTIBLE communicate information the reader may not know but needs to know. Reminders, by contrast, reiterate a message learned previously (often many times) or a message that is self-evident. Examples of reminders are CAUTION: STOP MACHINE BEFORE CLEANING and CAUTION: DO NOT REMOVE DRIVESHAFT GUARD.

Sometimes a multitude of safety signs or signs with lengthy lists of safety reminders are provided, apparently with the hope that all potentially unsafe, undesired practices will be covered. For many products, this hope is unfounded. For example, *any* powered machinery would require a list of over two dozen reminders simply to cover basic precautions that apply to all machines, such as DO NOT WEAR LOOSE CLOTHES, SHUT DOWN POWER BEFORE LEAVING MACHINE, KEEP WORK AREA CLEAN AND UNOBSTRUCTED, and so on. Reminders specific to the machine or job would add many more items to the list.

For some products the cost to the manufacturer of providing additional warnings on the product or in product literature is not a significant factor, and the ability to provide these warnings is virtually limitless. Designers in this situation face the question of how many reminders and traditional warnings to present and how often to repeat them.

The critical issue in any situation is *effectiveness*, that is, how well do safety signs prevent accidents. Several scientific studies have been conducted to explore this issue. The methods used involved observing human test subjects for any differences in their behavior based on the warnings they saw.

Unfortunately, all the research studies found little change in people's behavior after they read safety messages. (McCarthy et al, 1984) For messages that are best described as reminders, absolutely no positive change in human behavior was found in any of the studies. For messages best described as traditional warnings, behavior was affected either very little or not at all. (Friedman, 1988)

A recent study also explored how much attention people paid to warnings. Test subjects had to notice the warnings because they had to read directions that contained warning messages. The study revealed that 50% of the subjects read only the first few words—just enough to identify the message as a warning—then skipped to the next part of the directions, where they resumed reading. (Friedman, 1988) There are no comparable studies dating back to a time before it became common to place reminder messages on products. However, it is not unreasonable to speculate that the reason why 50% of the population chooses not to read warnings is that so many of these messages do not present any new information but are just reminders of well-known safety practices.

In addition, human factors and psychological studies have repeatedly proved that the human ability to distinguish among various stimuli decreases as the number of stimuli increases. The term "noise" has been coined to refer to a multitude of signals or messages that simultaneously compete for a person's attention. The greater the noise, the less likely that a particular message will get through. (Wickens, 1987) As Justice Warren Berger once said, "If we warn about everything, we warn about nothing."

Designers should consider these scientific findings when deciding which warnings and how many of them to put on a product. They must keep in mind that the more warning messages there are, the greater the noise. Unfortunately, the studies exploring this subject offer no hard and fast rules about what level of noise (i.e., number of warning messages) becomes counterproductive.

Because it has been shown that reminder messages have no effect on human behavior, designers should follow one definite rule: do not contribute to noise by using reminder safety messages if traditional safety messages can be displayed to the same audience in the same place or time. Because reminder messages are either useless or simply increase noise, they should be minimized or avoided, particularly when user safety depends on following one or more traditional safety messages.

Another scientific finding about warnings is that although they do not affect human behavior, they marginally affect users' perceptions of the product to which the warnings apply. Ironically, warnings increase people's perception of product quality while at the same time often increasing the perception of danger associated with the product, though only slightly.

Although the user's increased perception of danger does not translate into greater compliance with warning instructions, there may be some benefit to providing reminder warnings for new products. Modern products tend to have their inner workings encased in an outer shell that serves as an enclosure, a barrier guard, and an aesthetically pleasing shape. This shell might convey images of safety, simplicity, high technology, and so on. By contrast, the outward appearance of older products was largely dictated by their function, which meant that the inner workings of these machines were more visible. As a result, these products looked more threatening. There may be some benefit in placing reminder messages on modern products that appear safer than they really are. Users who read the messages might perceive these products as more risky. However, as yet there is no scientific evidence to prove that such a changed perception leads to safer behavior. There is even less hope for the effectiveness of reminders placed on older style products.

There is not always a clear distinction between what is an acceptable warning and what is merely a reminder. Designers in this situation who suspect they should provide reminder messages are likely to find the above criteria hazy about when such warnings should be provided. For guidance, designers should follow the same derived safety requirements (Table 3–1) as they do for designing all other aspects of products. Laws, regulations, and the other factors among derived safety requirements often address required warnings along with more functional safety requirements.

REFERENCES

Boggett WR and L Rodriquez. "On the Influence of a Perception of Danger on the Effectiveness of Warnings for Product Users." *Hazard Prevention,* July/Aug 1987.

Friedman K. "The Effect of Adding Symbols to Written Warning Labels on User Behavior and Recall." Santa Monica; CA: *Human Factors,* 30 (4), 1988, pp. 507–515.

McCarthy RL, et al. "Product Information Presentation, User Behavior, and Safety." *Proceedings of the Human Factors Society,* Vol. 1, 28th Annual Meeting. The Human Factors Society, Inc. 1984, pp. 81–85.

Wickens CD. "Information Processing, Decision Making and Cognition." In *Handbook of Human Factors,* New York: John Wiley and Sons, 1987, pp. 72–107.

5

Product Quality

The product safety professional must be as concerned with the manufacturing process as with the design process. This is particularly important for high-volume (low unit value) products because manufacturing defects are the more frequently alleged cause of injuries than are design defects. The product safety professional should be aware of all safety-critical phases of the manufacturing cycle, from the purchasing of components and/or raw materials through each step in the manufacturing and testing of each product. This chapter discusses the relationship between product safety and the manufacturing process.

Production and quality defects are major safety concerns for manufacturers of products. Because there is no successful defense for proven manufacturing defects, manufacturing personnel should be taught to appreciate the consequences of variances in product manufacturing that could lead to user injury. Such awareness training is a major concern of the product safety professional. It involves teaching workers to understand the concept of "criticality."

CRITICALITY

The most important safety-related quality control and production task is to identify safety-critical product components or attributes and to intensify quality control efforts on those aspects of the product. Because safety-critical components or attributes may not always be functionally critical as well, safety-critical parts may not be isolated routinely for vigorous inspection and testing by the quality control system. Quality control specialists should set up quality control plans for safety-critical parts or attributes. The specialists often can reduce manufacturing costs as well as improve safety and quality by using automated testing and statistical methods. When the company purchases identified safety-critical parts from others, the purchasing and quality control departments should practice a stringent level of qualification review in addition to the regular in-house quality efforts. The principal duties of those responsible for product safety are to:

1. Identify or confirm that others identify safety-critical parts or attributes (system safety techniques are often used for this purposes)

2. Ensure that the quality control department recognizes these safety-critical items, or criticalities, and appropriately deals with them.

A component or assembly may be critical because it is inherently hazardous (i.e., it is sensitive, damaging, or both; it has a high energy-release rate). Examples include explosive detonating devices, highly flammable liquid propellants, or tankage and combustion systems. A component may also be critical because its design has a single-point failure. That is, an accident could result from one component loss of function, human error, or one untimely, undesirable event. For example, one source of electrical power for both critical and non-critical electrical equipment could cause a failure of the whole system if there is an overload of noncritical electrical circuitry. High criticality also may be conferred because of foreseeable catastrophic failures that affect user safety. Examples include some loosened fasteners, certain snapped cables, and fatigued structural members.

Criticality ranking is a good tool to determine:

- Items that should be studied more to eliminate hazards that could cause failure, to check for fail-safe design, to reduce failure rate, or to contain damage

- Items that require special attention during production, require tight quality control, or need protective handling

- Special design, performance, reliability, safety, or quality assurance requirements that should be included in specifications to suppliers

- Special qualification/surveillance standards for vendors or subcontractors of critical components

- Parameters that need to be tested most intensively

- Special procedures, safeguards, protective equipment, monitoring devices, or warning systems that should be provided

- The most effective application of accident prevention efforts and funds

Identifying criticalities should be a major part of the design review process. Criticalities such as those cited previously are the result of a single failure and are readily identified by persons who understand the design and the nature of all its component parts. However, some criticalities arise because of the simultaneous or sequential failure of several component parts. For example, safety device A would fail if sensor 1 reads high and signaling circuit 2 fails to trigger. Such criticalities arise from a combination of failures. Because of the larger number of combinations of failures that theoretically could occur in a multi-component product, such criticalities are often difficult to recognize. Evaluating their likelihood and severity cannot be done by simple analysis. As a result, system safety techniques and design testing are employed to uncover such criticalities. (For a detailed discussion of system safety, see that section in Chapter 3, Product Design and Evaluation.) Software is available to facilitate criticality analysis.

PURCHASING POLICIES

The quality of materials purchased can significantly affect the safety of a company's products. The product safety professional should review the company's purchasing policies and procedures to determine their potential effects upon product safety. In particular, the professional should make sure that the following responsibilities are properly carried out:

- Preparing a "criticality list," i.e., a list of components and/or raw materials critical to product safety in cooperation with the engineering department

- Compiling a list of approved suppliers, using a vendor rating system developed in conjunction with the company's quality control department to rate the capabilities and reliability of suppliers

- Obtaining raw material and component lab reports, mill certifications, certificates of conformance, and other pertinent documents from suppliers specified by the engineering department

- Reviewing and analyzing the quality of components, parts, and raw materials to verify that they meet safety specifications

- Establishing a policy that any deviations from material specifications require the written permission of the engineering or design departments and a quality review board

Evaluation, Qualification, and Control of Suppliers

It can be just as important to control the quality of materials and services purchased from vendors as it is to establish and enforce internal quality control (particularly in recent years with the trends toward more outsourcing and "just-in-time" inventory control). The degree and extent of the quality controls established for a supplier depend upon the criticality of the supplier's product and the known capabilities and reliability of the supplier. That is, quality controls and checks should be far more extensive for highly critical components and for new suppliers with no proven quality history. The most effective requirement is to choose suppliers who can maintain adequate quality. Another vital factor is open, active, and adequate flow of information between the company and its suppliers.

Note:
It is unwise in the absence of proper supplier qualification and surveillance to rely solely upon supplier quality control procedures. The manufacturer is ultimately responsible for defects in purchased raw materials, parts, assemblies, services, and other items provided by vendors. Should a component part from a supplier cause an accident, the manufacturer is likely to be unsuccessful in transferring damages to the supplier if it can be shown that the manufacturer did not use reasonable care to discover defects in purchased items, if the identity of the supplier cannot be established, or if the supplier goes out of business. Manufacturers should try to obtain from suppliers a certificate of product liability insurance as well as an indemnification and hold harmless agreement.

Control and verification of the quality of supplied materials can be assured by using the following methods.

Supplier Planning
The company must furnish suppliers with detailed requirements to avoid misunderstanding or misinterpretation. The three areas involved in this planning are:

- *Purchasing Instructions*
  Instructions to the purchasing department must include configuration data, quality requirements, and general data concerning supplier control.

- *Supplier Instructions*
  The purchasing department must pass along to the supplier the configuration data, quality requirements, and supplier control data it received.

- *Inspection Instructions*
  The instructions must indicate whether inspection is to be made at the source or by the receiving inspection personnel, and at what stages.

Supplier Surveillance

The object of surveillance is to determine which suppliers consistently produce high quality work and to reward them with prompt payment and new orders. The supplier with an effective quality control system permits the buyer to reduce inspection. There are five methods of maintaining surveillance:

- *Vendor Qualification Audits*
  Before placing purchase orders, quality control personnel should survey the vendor facilities to determine the adequacy of the vendor quality control system.

- *Engineering-Approved Sources*
  Based upon successful test data, engineering will specify a particular product from a specific source and prohibit the substitution of a similar (or "equal") product from another source.

- *Source and Receiving Inspection*
  Results of inspection by source and receiving inspection personnel immediately indicate the effectiveness of the vendor quality control system.

- *Resident Representatives*
  A company may choose to maintain its own employee at the vendor's site to inspect every step of the manufacturing process of the supplier.

- *Performance Records*
  Both supplier records and independent testing laboratory records should be obtained wherever possible.

MANUFACTURING POLICIES

After a reasonably safe and reliable product has been designed, it must be turned into a finished product. Certain steps of the manufacturing process are likely to be more important than others because some errors in manufacturing—errors in safety-critical product components or attributes—could result in an unsafe and unreliable product.

The manufacturing department can contribute to an overall product safety program in many ways. By evaluating the manufacturing department policies and procedures, the product safety professional can assess its contribution. The professional should ask:

- Do manufacturing personnel understand what tasks are safety critical?

- Does the manufacturing department motivate its employees by taking steps to make sure that all employees understand they are making a vital contribution to the quality and safety (where applicable) of the products?

- Does the manufacturing department provide effective and supervised on-the-job training procedures?

- Does the manufacturing department have a continuous quality improvement program, such as statistical process controls?

- Does the manufacturing department implement zero defects or error-free performance or other preventive action programs?

- Is there a program or procedure to control product irregularities affecting quality or safety? (This would normally be accomplished in conjunction with the inspection and testing personnel of the quality control department. Quality assurance is discussed in the next section of this chapter.)

- Do appropriate personnel have the necessary engineering education?

- Are there adequate employee education and literacy?

- Are there plant facilities capable of proper reproduction of the design?

- Is there a policy to prohibit unauthorized deviations from design specifications and work procedures?

- Do manufacturing personnel participate in safety reviews on new product designs by serving on the product safety committee, if one exists, or on design review committees?

Sometimes product requirements cannot be achieved with the level of expertise, materials, machines, or equipment currently in the shop. When this situation occurs and the component is safety critical, the production department must advise the design engineering department of the problem. The integrity of safety-critical parts should not be sacrificed to maintain cost or to retain work that should be contracted to an outside firm. Sometimes production problems can be solved by deviating from specifications. If deviations are necessary or unavoidable, they should be made only with the approval of the designers to ensure that product safety is not thereby compromised. Inability to manufacture a product as designed is one reason manufacturing personnel should be involved early in the design process. Usually there are many small changes that manufacturers would prefer in a design. If these changes are made early in the design process, they are much easier to accomplish.

QUALITY ASSURANCE

The terms "quality assurance" or "quality control" refer broadly to that function of company management where calculated actions are taken to ensure that all products conform to internal design or engineering requirements. At one time, the terms "quality assurance" and "statistical quality assurance" were considered synonymous because statistical techniques were regarded as the major tools of quality assurance. Over the years, however, quality assurance has taken on a larger meaning to include whatever actions are necessary to ensure that products not only conform to design, but to external customer requirements and to customer expectations and satisfaction.

One of the most important requirements for the effective operation of a quality assurance program is the company's positive interest and concern, which starts at the top level of management. In most instances, quality assurance responsibilities must be delegated. The assignment of responsibility and authority should be clearly defined throughout all levels of management, supervision, and operations.

Evaluating the Overall Quality Assurance System

To help the product safety professional assess the adequacy of quality assurance efforts, the following list itemizes ways that quality assurance personnel contribute to product safety:

- Assist in identifying safety-critical parts or attributes while also making sure that defective products do not leave the facility.

- Prepare a quality assurance system with appropriate provisions for safety-critical parts or attributes.

- Assign special quality requirements for safety-critical parts.

- Develop procedures to identify and eliminate important production trouble spots. This should be accomplished in conjunction with manufacturing personnel.

- Work with the engineering or design department to set minimum acceptable product quality standards.

- Operate as an independent and objective group regarding key product parameters. (The quality assurance department should report at the same level as the manufacturing, engineering or design, and marketing departments and should operate on a budget that is its own. The head of the company quality assurance activity should participate in top management meetings and decision making.)

- Maintain key quality assurance records for appropriate lengths of time, particularly for critical parts and components.

It is important to determine whether the quality assurance system is adequate to carry out the quality objectives of the company and whether it functions as planned. To evaluate a quality assurance system effectively, the product safety professional should thoroughly review the implementation of key elements of the system, including these items:

- Quality assurance policies and procedures

- Engineering/product design coordination

- Control of suppliers/vendors

- Manufacturing quality (in-process and final assembly)

- Special process control

- Measuring equipment calibration system

- Sample inspection procedures

- Nonconforming material procedures

- Material status/storage system

- Corrective and preventive action systems

- Product preservation, packaging, and shipping procedures

- Record retention system

- Training procedures

- Testing system

- Quality assurance internal audit system evaluation

- Document control system

Manuals

In all organizations, there should be a quality control manual, the form and content of which will vary according to company requirements. The manual is usually divided into three sections: policy, procedures, and detailed work instructions.

Policy

The policy section should achieve the following:

- States company quality assurance policy and objectives

- Establishes organizational responsibilities

- Establishes systems for implementing quality assurance policy

Procedures

The procedures section should accomplish the following:

- States operational responsibilities

- Gives detailed operating instructions

- Gives method to evaluate testing system

Work Instructions

The work instructions section provides detailed, step-by-step instructions for how tasks are to be accomplished.

The policy section of the manual is usually a general discussion of quality assurance functions. The procedures section, on the other hand, contains the daily detailed operations of the quality assurance department and may include the quality assurance duties of others in the organization.

PRODUCT TESTING

The tests performed on products can be categorized into two types: design validation testing and quality (or batch) testing. Design validation testing refers to tests done to evaluate whether a new design performs its functions and meets other requirements as intended by the designers. Such tests are mostly conducted during prototype development, although they also may include a long-term testing program to detect changes in products' performance capabilities caused by worn-out tooling, new tooling, new component suppliers, and so on. Design tests tend to be done on an as-needed or project basis, and may involve outside independent laboratories.

Quality, or batch, testing refers to tests performed on manufactured products and assemblies and components to ensure that products conform to the design. These tests tend to be done daily as a routine part of production. Usually, manufacturers conduct these tests in-house. The major exception is when a product requires certification by an independent authority. In this case, routine internal quality testing is supplemented by an independent testing organization.

In short, design testing validates the design, and quality testing validates the manufacture. Typically, both types of testing are planned by quality control professionals and may share some of the same testing techniques used for particular products. However, the goals for each test are different; therefore, different testing programs are necessary.

Design Testing

Many products undergo design testing, but not mainly for product safety reasons. Nevertheless, one class of products, such as aviation components, smoke detectors, safety belts, and so on, must function correctly in order to ensure user safety. For these products any design defect is not only a source of user dissatisfaction, but also a hazard to the user. Thus, the product safety professional should ensure that expert, prototype, and ongoing design testing programs are established. Such a design testing program probably would include:

- Prototype sample testing

- Tool capability analysis

- Process capability testing

- Review of all drawings for completeness, consistency, and conformance to specifications

- Layout inspection of parts produced by molds and other special tools

- Automatic electronic testing of software

- Long-term permanent performance testing

- Testing of packaging for adequate product protection, if applicable

- Review of markings and labels for products such as drugs for statements of shelf life

Another class of products, such as machine tools, has safety-critical parts or attributes, but these criticalities constitute only a small portion of the total product. In this situation, those particular safety-critical parts or attributes should be studied during design testing.

For nonsafety-critical aspects, the manufacturer's testing activities can be concentrated on the "traditional" concerns of the design-testing function. Once a new product has been introduced, the manufacturer is interested in testing the actual product performance characteristics against design objectives for marketing considerations and to avoid problems with advertising and sales claims. The manufacturer is also interested in estimating the percentage of products that may fail prior to the expiration of the guarantee or warranty period in order to estimate the probable costs of guarantees and warranties.

Many companies are aware of the benefits of employing quality and design-testing professionals who can apply testing technology to enhance product performance and safety and thus reduce costs.

Quality Testing

Quality testing refers to tests and inspections conducted to determine whether established requirements are met (Figures 5–1 and 5–2). This type of testing usually includes one or more of the following general methods employed during and after manufacture:

- Visual inspection

- Dimensional inspection

- Hardness testing

- Functional testing

- Nondestructive testing (NDT)

- Chemical/metallurgical testing

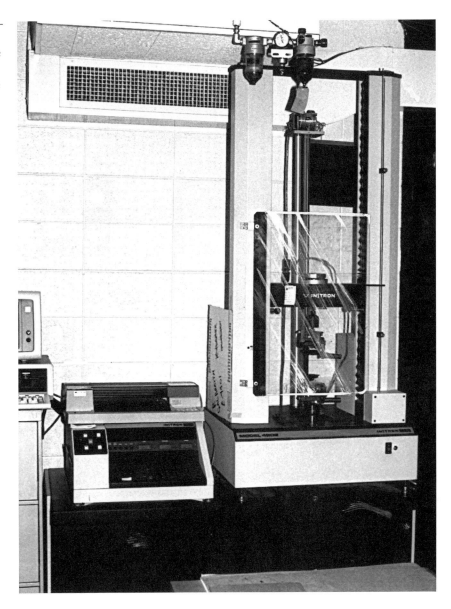

Figure 5–1.
This tensile testing equipment tests the strength of a product. Notice that the safety shield of the equipment must be in place before operating the tester.

Figure 5–2.
This Rockwell hardness tester is used for checking adherence to metal hardness specification.

Evaluation of Testing Program

It is the responsibility of the quality assurance department, using a number of internal testing procedures, to ensure that desired product quality levels are achieved and maintained and that scrap and rework are kept to a minimum by the manufacturing department.

The first step in setting up an effective testing program is to determine which categories of testing are appropriate for the products involved. Except for the simplest of products, it is highly advantageous to have quality and design testing programs devised by professional level and/or test engineering personnel. Persons knowledgeable in test instrumentation, statistical quality methods, and other fields within the quality assurance discipline can provide the maximum benefits for the time and money invested. Although reviewing the field of quality assurance is beyond the scope of this book, the basic categories of testing are given in Figure 5–3. The most common testing categories are acceptance, conformance, and performance testing.

In a satisfactory testing environment, the product safety professional should see the following evidence of test planning:

- Names of the tests

- Statements of the test purposes and objectives

- Descriptions of the sample sizes required, if appropriate

- Descriptions of the sampling methods to be used, if appropriate

- Descriptions of any special test sample preparation required

- Specifications for the test equipment and ancillary materials needed

- Definition of the details of the test methods to be employed

- Name, date and authority of the person or persons performing the test

Figure 5–3.
Categories of quality
assurance testing.

Acceptance and Conformance Testing

The primary issue is whether the products or components being tested meet given specifications.

Acceptance Testing
- Raw materials
- Components
- Subassemblies

Conformance Testing
- Dimensions
- Physical and chemical characteristics

Control Testing

The concern is whether the methods, machines, equipment, or processes being used by the company are adequate to perform their intended objectives.

- Tools
- Jigs and fixtures
- Machinery
- Processes
- Test equipment

Assurance Testing

The concern is whether the quality (usually expressed as a percentage) of product output fully meets the advertised specifications or marketing claims. Assurance testing applies only to higher volume products.

- Processes
- Products

Performance Testing

The company compares the tested products' actual performance with specifications, desired level of performance, or alternative products. Major examples include "hi-pot" tests (a high-voltage breakdown test) and ground continuity testing.

- Life tests
- Endurance tests
- Guarantee and warranty tests
- Comparison tests
- Overstress tests

INDEPENDENT TESTING

Types of product testing that a company cannot do or cannot do economically can be contracted to an independent testing laboratory. Many testing laboratories offer highly specialized testing services, such as:

- Determination of physical characteristics, such as abrasion resistance or weathering

- Testing of mechanical and electrical parameters for particular product classes

- Fracture mechanics and metallurgy

- Chemical analyses

- Nondestructive testing, including x-ray, ultrasonic, and magnetic particle examination

- Computerized electronics testing

- Testing of thermal and flammability characteristics

- Nuclear and radiological testing

- Toxicology and other biological testing

Sometimes a company should consider the services of an independent testing laboratory even when the company has the capacity to do the tests in-house. Outside testing may be mandated by code, specification, or the rules of a regulatory agency. This is particularly true when a product must be certified that it meets certain government specifications. Approximately 40 laboratories in the United States have been authorized to grant such certifications. The independent laboratory also may play an important role in a voluntary trade association program for certification and labeling. In some cases, a company's concern about potential litigation issues may cause it to use an independent laboratory. Finally, the independent laboratory may lend credibility and objectivity to product performance-substantiation programs.

In certain instances, companies having superior testing capabilities should consider certifying on their own authority and reputation that their products comply with existing standards. If no standards exist, they could certify that their products comply with an appropriate standard that the company has developed and documented.

PRODUCT DOCUMENTATION AND CHANGE CONTROL

To implement any effective quality assurance program properly, the company should require that 100% complete design drawings and performance specifications of any product be established prior to manufacturing start-up. Otherwise, there is an inadequate basis for testing or inspection, and parts of the design process are likely to be done on the assembly floor or at the suppliers' facilities. In either case, part of the design would be out of the safety professional's control. The persons responsible for product safety should make sure that a system is in place in either the manufacturing, engineering, or production department that will trigger an automatic notice should the design be incomplete.

Records

The company should maintain records for the manufacturing operations and quality assurance procedures, including incoming materials, assemblies or processes, and final inspection results. Manufacturing nonconformances must not be tolerated except with the approval of design engineering and a quality review board. Documentation of such approvals is mandatory. (Record retention will be covered in greater detail in Chapter 8, Record Retention Requirements.)

Special Process Control

Because manufacturing processes greatly influence the fitness of the completed product, it is imperative that the process be positively, yet economically, controlled. Usually, conducting a 100% inspection of all product characteristics is not feasible because it might require destructive testing to determine conformance. Therefore, controls should be designed to monitor and to ensure that similarly processed items will meet desired quality standards. Some processes used to change the physical, mechanical, chemical, or dimensional characteristics of materials to make a product include, but are not limited to, the following:

- Heat treating
- Plating
- Fusion welding
- Stamping and forming
- Batch mixing
- Chemical mixing
- Adhesive bonding

Processes are controlled as follows. (1) Quality assurance staff review and approve the manufacturing procedures, detailed instructions, set-up procedures, and controls. (2) The staff conduct audits periodically to verify that manufacturing is processing the work in accordance with established procedure. (3) The staff use various methods to control the processes to make sure that completed products comply with processing standards and requirements.

Calibration of Measuring Equipment

Measuring and process control equipment and instruments used to ensure that manufactured products and processes conform to specified requirements must be calibrated periodically. In other words, any equipment used, either directly or indirectly, to measure, control, or record should be calibrated against certified standards so that the equipment may be adjusted, replaced, or repaired before it becomes inaccurate. Some typical measuring devices are:

- Micrometers
- Calipers
- Surface plates
- Hardness testers
- Tensile testers
- Level indicators
- Pressure-measuring devices
- Temperature gauges
- Voltmeters
- Ammeters
- Recording instruments
- Electronic gauges

Equipment subject to periodic calibration should include equipment used by quality assurance personnel and devices used by manufacturing personnel in controlling an operation. The latter also includes personally owned equipment where employees provide their own measuring devices to determine conformance or nonconformance.

Statistical Sampling

Statistical sampling refers to techniques used by quality assurance personnel to ascertain the quality of a lot without inspecting or testing all items in the lot. It can be a beneficial tool if used correctly, but it can be a problem if misused. Statistical samples can be very complex and are usually designed by quality assurance professionals.

Contrary to common opinion, 100% inspection and testing of products performed under the most favorable conditions does not ensure 100% quality. This is the case because human, mechanical, and other types of errors are impossible to eliminate totally. However, a properly planned and implemented, statistically based sampling technique can produce highly satisfactory results. This is true despite the fact that, occasionally, statistical sampling does not give a true picture of the quality of a particular lot—good lots can be rejected or bad lots can be accepted. Professionals in this field know how to design sampling systems that achieve specified, desired quality levels.

The level of quality desired in a sampling plan is normally expressed as an acceptable quality level (AQL) value, also referred to as the quality index. The standard definition of AQL is a nominal value expressed in terms of percent of defective units or defects per hundred units, whichever is applicable. The most widely used standard sampling tables are those issued by the U.S. government and contained in the publication "Sampling Procedures and Tables for Inspection by Attributes." (MIL–STD–105, Revision E, 1989)

Companies should maintain sampling records that show at least part number, lot quantity, sample size, AQL value, and inspection results.

Nonconforming Material Control Procedures

The term "nonconforming material" is usually applied to products that are rejected because they do not meet established requirements. Raw material, parts, components, subassemblies, and assemblies become nonconforming material at whatever manufacturing stage they begin to vary from the standards.

The company should have a system to control nonconforming material. It should include the following:

Identification
The status of all nonconforming material must be immediately identified and clearly labeled with a tag, form, or other marking so that it is readily seen. A nonconforming material record showing the discrepancies in detail should be kept.

Segregation
After identification, all nonconforming material should be segregated from acceptable material and placed in a separate area pending disposition. When nonconforming material cannot be moved to the separate area, the material must be clearly identified to prevent its inadvertent use.

Disposition
Disposition of nonconforming material must be made by authorized personnel—at a minimum, the engineering or design department and quality control department representatives. In some instances, other department representatives may be authorized to act in conjunction with the authorized engineering or design and quality assurance personnel, or the customer may specify that disposition of nonconforming material must have his or her approval.

Reinspection
Nonconforming material that has been reworked or repaired must be inspected afterwards to make sure that it conforms to both the disposition and original parameters before being accepted.

Customer Notification
The system for handling nonconforming material must include procedures for submitting, when required, the discrepant material and proposed disposition to the customer for approval. The customer may or may not approve the disposition.

Supplier Reporting

The nonconforming material system must include procedures for subcontractors to report nonconforming material to the company. The company will decide on the disposition of the material and send the supplier a copy of its report.

Records

The company must maintain records of all nonconforming discrepancies, dispositions, and results of reinspection.

Material Status and Storage

The company must have a way to know at all times whether a product (or lot) has not been inspected, has been inspected and approved, or has been inspected and rejected. All raw materials, components, sub-assemblies, assemblies, and end products should bear identification of their current manufacturing process, inspection, and test status.

The material storage function involves the temporary holding of raw materials and recently purchased or in-process parts and assemblies. Storage personnel must have a control system that indicates at all times the status and the condition of stored raw materials, components, and products.

The product safety professional must evaluate the effectiveness of the controls used by the company to make sure that the stock on hand is the stock ordered, and that the system used to identify the materials in the storeroom is adequate. The product safety professional should also verify the adequacy of procedures for segregating stock into specific areas (such as "Material awaiting receiving inspection or test sample results," "Accepted materials," and "Rejected materials") and procedures that control which employees are authorized to withdraw material.

All stored material should be controlled by a material identification system such as color coding, tagging, or material stamping. When material is either lying on the ground, in the aisles, in the wrong racks, or in a congested area, there is a strong possibility that workers are using inadequate control and identification procedures.

Corrective and Preventive Action Systems

The corrective action system is a follow-up of the nonconforming material system. The objective of this system is to use the discrepancies reported in the nonconforming material system to perform the following tasks:

• Analyze manufacturing errors.

• Send requests for corrective action to the party responsible for the errors, evaluate responses, and determine the effectiveness of the action taken.

• Analyze manufacturing rejection rates and report to management the dollar losses due to scrap, rework/repair, and reinspection costs.

• Anticipate potential causes of nonconformance and prevent their occurrence.

PACKAGING, HANDLING, SHIPPING, AND DISTRIBUTION

Before a completed product is shipped to a customer, quality assurance personnel should observe these important safety considerations:

• The product shipped is, in fact, the product the customer expects.

• The product is properly preserved.

• The product is adequately packaged according to applicable standards to prevent shipping or handling damage.

• Required warnings and handling and opening instructions are on or in the package.

• Shipping papers, parts lists, manuals, warranties, certification, and other required safety- or health-related data are included in the shipment.

• Records of products shipped; identification data, if any; the receiver; and other pertinent data are maintained.

• Hazardous packaging and disposal instructions are identified—this can be documented on film or other media.

Packaging for any product must meet standard specifications. The U.S. Department of Transportation sets these specifications, and it is particularly important to follow them when hazardous materials are involved (see 49 *CFR* 173 and 178). Shipping containers should be tested to make sure they comply with applicable regulations (Figures 5–4, 5–5).

Figure 5–4.
This incline impact tester is used to simulate railroad car impacts on a product being shipped. Such tests ensure that the product packaging will protect the product during shipping and prevent defects that could lead to product safety problems.

Figure 5–5.
This vibration test equipment simulates the vibrations that packages receive during shipping.

RECORD-KEEPING SYSTEMS

Because of their volume, records can be a troublesome by-product of quality assurance, but they also can be a useful end-product. Records document the history of a product and can verify that the company's quality assurance system functioned as planned to inspect and/or test the product. (See Chapter 8, Record Retention Requirements, and Chapter 10, Risk Management, for more details.)

Good quality assurance records also help track products and can include:

- Lists of raw materials from which products are produced

- Inspection results for purchased and manufactured products

- Inspection results from each inspection station

- Special processes control data

- Calibration data

- Sample inspection data

- Nonconforming material data

- Error analysis and corrective action data

- Shipping data

Ideally, records that relate to safety-critical parts or attributes should be carefully stored for one of the following periods, whichever is longer: the likely maximum life of the product or the period required by legal or regulatory considerations.

REFERENCES

Crosby PB. *Quality Is Free: The Art of Making Quality Decisions*. New York: McGraw-Hill, 1979.

MIL–STD–105, Revision E, Washington, DC: Department of Defense, May 1989.

6 Marketing and Sales Activities

After a company has designed and manufactured a safe product, it may incur unnecessary product complaints by the manner in which the product is represented to customers and users. This chapter discusses sales training, advertising and marketing literature, media advertising, and public relations. In these areas the product safety professional should check that printed or pictured materials encourage safe use of the product.

SALES TRAINING

The product safety professional should review the manner in which the company's products are distributed and marketed. In other words, are they distributed and sold through dealers, direct sales, manufacturing representatives, wholesalers, distributors, retail stores, mail order outlets, or other marketing channels? Are products going to private label reformulators, to assemblers of final product, or to companies or users overseas? What is the level of specialization, sophistication, and control over the distributors and sellers? Finally, are franchised dealers, company-owned stores, or large chains of retail stores involved in product sales? This review must be made in order to evaluate properly whether the advertising and sales literature, warranties and disclaimers, sales record retention activities, and advertising sales personnel training procedures are effective regarding the type of product marketing techniques used.

The company must also be able to verify that its sales personnel and dealers have been instructed to describe accurately the capabilities and the consequences of misuse of the products they are selling or distributing. The company should be able to prove that it has tried to avoid incurring undesired implied and/or expressed warranties. For example, sales personnel must be instructed not to exaggerate the capabilities of the company products.

The product safety professional also should review the marketing department's policies regarding retention (for the life of the product) of sales and distribution records that can be used to identify purchasers. These records can help a company implement product recall or field-modification programs. In addition, these records should indicate, whenever possible, the use to which the company products will be put, particularly when they are sold to subcontractors or assemblers.

Finally, the coordinator must accurately determine whether marketing activities include leasing or renting products to dealers, distributors, contractors, or customers. If so, the company must recognize that it is generally difficult to maintain satisfactory control over the maintenance and repair procedures used for leased or rented products unless the company carefully plans to monitor these procedures. Furthermore, the quality of maintenance, service, repair, and operating instructions becomes more significant for leased or rented products than it does under normal sales circumstances.

ADVERTISING AND MARKETING LITERATURE

Customers often rely on the sales personnel, advertising, sales brochures, and operating, service, and maintenance instructions for their knowledge of the product capabilities and limitations. Advertising and marketing literature is the manufacturer's first opportunity to guide the user's expectations before purchase toward the intended use of the product. If the customer is led to believe that the product has capabilities it does not possess and such belief leads to an accident, an injured customer may have legal cause for action where none existed before. The product safety program coordinator should review the advertising and marketing materials, which should show the following characteristics:

- Be clear and accurate

- Not overstate product capabilities

- Not encourage the customer to believe the product has uses for which it was not designed nor intended

- State only what the product can do safely

- Show only safe operating procedures

- Show the product only with safety devices in place

- Be reviewed and approved by the design and legal departments to ensure accuracy and to verify safety implications

- Show the user appropriately dressed and wearing proper personal protective equipment for the job

The use of broad, absolute descriptive terms, such as "moisture-proof," "absolutely safe," "tamper-proof," "completely nontoxic," and the like, often may be interpreted as an unjustified overstatement of product capabilities and may lead to an unwarranted feeling of safety on the part of the product user. Instead, terms such as "moisture-resistant" or "tamper-resistant" are more appropriate for use in advertising and marketing literature because they more clearly define the actual capabilities of the product. Furthermore, should the need arise, these terms can be defended more easily in a court of law.

The company should not advertise its products as having "safety" components or attributes that provide unqualified or complete safety. Instead, it should be stated that the particular component or attribute is intended to reduce or control the hazard involved in the use of the product.

Warranties and Disclaimers

The product safety professional should review warranties and disclaimers (Figure 6–1). They should be:

- Reasonable and practical for the uses intended

- Clear and concise

- Prominently displayed and easily recognizable by the customer or product user

- Thoroughly reviewed by the legal department or legal counsel to ensure compliance with all jurisdictions in which the product is to be sold

Figure 6–1.
This sample warranty is clear, concise, reasonable, and highly visible.

WARRANTY

XYZ Corporation warrants that the new ABC Model EC209, EC212, ECS209, or ECS212 strapping tool will be free from defects in material and workmanship for a period of ninety (90) days after the date of its delivery to the owner's place of business. XYZ's sole liability hereunder will be to repair or replace without charge, f.o.b. Anywhere, Illinois, plant, any part which proves to be defective within such period. However, XYZ reserves the right to replace any tool proven to contain a defect with a rebuilt tool of the same model if in XYZ's judgment such replacement is appropriate to efficiently cure the defect. Any rebuilt tool provided the owner in accordance with this warranty will carry a warranty for the balance of the period of warranty applicable to the tool it replaces. This warranty is void as to any tool that has been subjected to misuse, accident, or negligent damage, repaired with other than genuine XYZ replacement parts, damaged in transit or handling, or which in XYZ's opinion has been altered or repaired in a way that affects or detracts from the performance of the tool.

XYZ CORPORATION MAKES NO WARRANTY, EXPRESS OR IMPLIED, RELATING TO MERCHANTABILITY, FITNESS OR OTHERWISE EXCEPT AS STATED ABOVE AND XYZ CORPORATION'S LIABILITY AS ASSUMED ABOVE IS IN LIEU OF ALL OTHERS ARISING OUT OF OR IN CONNECTION WITH THE USE AND PERFORMANCE OF THE TOOL. It is expressly understood that XYZ Corporation shall in no event be liable for any indirect or consequential damages including, but not limited to, damages that may arise from loss of anticipated profits or production, spoilage of materials, increased costs of operation, or otherwise.

Companies should never consider disclaimers of liability as a substitute for proper product design. Furthermore, all disclaimers have four important limitations:

1. The effect of disclaimers is generally limited to the parties in contractual agreement, which often does not include the injured user.

2. "Unconscionable" disclaimers (against public policy, unreasonable, unfair, impractical, unscrupulous), are not enforceable. Many courts will not give legal effect to overly broad disclaimers, as they may seem to be a paper substitute for appropriate safe design.

3. Some federal statutes impose criminal liability on a seller for failure to give warning of known hazards, regardless of any effort to disclaim liability.

4. Disclaimers are most effective when used formally between relatively equal parties, such as between one company and another. They are less likely to be enforced if they are between an individual and a large company.

Instruction and Sales Literature

The instruction manual and/or video should assist in fulfilling the company's obligation to educate the user about the proper use of the product. If instruction manuals do not adequately warn users of a product's hazards and an accident occurs, an injured user may have legal cause for action where none existed before.

Instruction manuals that accompany the products should repeat hazard warnings as well as describe how the hazards may be reduced or avoided. In addition, instructions should be given on how to inspect the product upon receipt and how to assemble, install, and inspect it periodically. If the manuals include troubleshooting hints, the dangers involved should be explained. For example, the use of unauthorized parts, the removal of a back panel, and the presence of hazardous energy sources are some of the dangers that should be discussed. Also, the manual should include information on the required preventive maintenance program and disposal of waste materials. (See Chapter 4 for more details on instruction manuals.)

Sales brochures and product advertising should be reviewed by the engineering or design department and legal counsel to be sure the product capabilities are depicted accurately. They should also be reviewed by the product safety authority to ensure they show only safe operating and maintenance procedures. Service contracts should be reviewed to be sure that the service provided is clearly stated.

Distribution of Product Literature

When product literature contains safety information, both the content of the product and its physical distribution to the purchasers are equally important. Those responsible for product safety should review company practices for placing literature in the hands of the user. Several examples of common distribution methods are given below.

When safety-related manuals are not physically attached to the product, it is important to document the procedures for making sure that the accompanying literature does, in fact, reach the user. Good practice for some products includes quality control procedures to make sure the literature is enclosed within the product package. For example, some companies even attach literature to products so it is virtually impossible for the product to be received by the user without its literature.

For low-volume, high-value industrial products, good practice includes confirmation letters to the buyer stating the literature was provided. At least one industrial product manufacturer has gone so far as to attach the operator's manual by a chain to the machine. Another manufacturer places instructions in a drawer on the machine. Some companies put part numbers on manuals along with ordering information to make it easy to reorder new manuals if they become damaged or if more are needed.

If more safety-related information becomes available, appropriate literature should be rewritten and distributed to customers and users to fulfill the company's retroactive or ongoing duty to warn users of potential hazards. Many companies send free safety bulletins, notices, updated warning decals, and retrofit kits to customers of high-value products.

SAFETY EQUIPMENT

Those responsible for product safety may be faced with demands to delete costly safety devices or to make them extra-cost options. They may be told that "safety doesn't sell," an axiom heard not only from sales people but also, unfortunately, from some authors of marketing textbooks. In the marketing literature, products whose main purpose or advantage is to prevent undesired events such as accidents fall into the category of "undesired goods," a category characterized as requiring intensive (i.e., costly) marketing efforts.

In years past, manufacturers of products that had a safety advantage but a resulting competitive cost disadvantage could address the problem by making safety devices or features optional. This solution was viable when negligence law formed the basis of most product liability lawsuits. Imprudent buyers who refused to purchase optional safety features and who suffered injury from an accident were unlikely to succeed in a lawsuit against the manufacturer or seller.

Today, however, strict liability has replaced negligence law as the basis of many lawsuits against the manufacturer. Under strict liability, only the product itself is at issue; the actions of the buyer and seller are irrelevant. Manufacturers who offer a safety feature as an optional extra-cost item only prove that a safer product was, in fact, feasible. The product must be free of defect at the time of sale.

Note:
Many safety features are no longer optional but mandatory under the regulations of the jurisdiction in which the product is sold.

In some instances, however, companies can provide optional safety features. For products that are reasonably safe with standard equipment, additional safety devices may be sold as extra-cost options. For example, automobiles can be sold with regular brakes as standard equipment and with antilock braking systems offered as an extra-cost option. The decision about which safety devices to include and what should be offered as options must be made carefully. Such decisions may well become the subject of litigation, as has happened with the automakers' decisions on air-bag installations. Some products having many distinct purposes or usages may have a safety device that is applicable to only one usage. Such a device may not necessarily be standard equipment for all users. For example, paper-cutting machines meant to be loaded by automatic feeding devices are provided with a safety curtain in front of the knife; manually fed machines are provided with two-hand safety control devices. If these two modes of operation are not likely to be used interchangeably on the same machine, it may not be necessary for both sets of safety devices to be provided with each machine.

MEDIA ADVERTISING

Televised advertisements require attention-getting, dramatic action. This may make it more difficult to avoid exaggerating the capabilities or suggesting unwanted or unsafe uses of the product. These two factors—the audience and "artistic license—make it both more important and more difficult for the product safety professional to monitor media advertising.

The potential problems related to televised advertisements include:

• Overuse of dramatic action

• Showing unsafe practices

• Showing behaviors in which participants are not wearing appropriate personal protective equipment

To illustrate the potential problems, consider an experience of the automobile industry. In a recent lawsuit the plaintiff argued that because televised advertisements showed utility and off-road vehicles being driven fast over hilly terrain and sand dunes, the company was implying that it was safe to drive their product in such a manner. In real life, however, one of the vehicles overturned and injured the occupants. The advertisement showed a stunt driver using the vehicle in a way that would be unsafe usage for an ordinary driver. It is ill-advised to show misuses of products or uses that cannot be duplicated safely by the ordinary user.

PUBLIC RELATIONS

In any public relations program, it is just as important, if not more so, to know *what not to do* as it is to know *what to do*. Many companies maintain a public relations department to handle any product-related news event, including a product recall or a major accident. If this is the case, the product safety professional should ask that department what specific assistance he to she can give. If, however, the company has no public relations spokesperson and the product safety professional deals directly with the media, the following cardinal rules apply:

1. Have a plan for dealing with the media.

2. Publicize good news.

3. Do not avoid, delay, duck, cover up, or deny bad news.

4. Be ready to put a favorable twist on bad news if there is some good that could result from the event.

Handling Good News

Whenever a company does something unusual to promote product safety, the media should be notified. For example, if the company sponsors a community group distributing product safety information or conducts safe usage talks before school groups, community groups, or labor or trade union groups, notify the media in advance. If a company advances the state of the art in a safety feature of a product, write a news release and send it to the appropriate newspaper city editors and radio or TV news directors.

The following points may help a product safety professional deal successfully with the media:

1. Be honest in what you say. Never exaggerate or claim to have achieved absolute safety in a product.

2. Deliver what you promise. Deliver any written material, photos, or videotapes on the date due.

3. If an announced event is canceled or rescheduled, notify the media at once.

4. Be accurate in all facts, names, places, and dates given.

5. Send news releases or a letter outlining the event; do not telephone unless the situation is an emergency.

6. Send all information and materials a week or two before the date of the event.

7. Do not suggest that a news crew or reporter be sent out; that is the news director's decision.

8. Do not write propaganda for the company. Just give the facts regarding who, what, when, where, how, and why as concisely as possible.

9. If sending a photo, write a caption on a separate paper and tape it to the back or bottom of the photo. Do not use paper clips or write with pen or pencil on the back of the photo.

Handling Bad News

Every manufacturer or retailer of products should have a plan for dealing with the media in the event of a major product safety-related accident or product recall (see also Recall Preparedness in Chapter 9). One key element of the plan should be to name the company spokesperson who is to deal with the media. All other company personnel should refer media representatives to that individual.

Regardless of whether the product safety professional is the person chosen to deal with the media, the following points will help the spokesperson handle the situation successfully:

1. Check with legal counsel in advance of the incident or the interview, if possible, about what information can be given in a press interview.

2. Do not deny obvious facts but do not express opinions or conclusions about who or what is responsible for the accident. Do not speculate.

3. Answer questions factually, but briefly. Remember that there is no such thing as "off the record."

4. Emphasize good points about the product safety record or awards of the company.

5. Control nervous habits—look directly at the camera or interviewer; speak clearly and without haste; do not fidget—look relaxed and in control.

6. Give important details to product users (such as product identification number, in the case of a recall) or relatives (in the case of an accident). Remember that details of any casualties must be given privately and personally to next-of-kin first, before releasing such information to the news media.

7. Make a practice videotape before any event happens and critique it for nervous mannerisms, body language, and projection of confidence.

No one wants to deal with bad news, but as in all situations in life, foresight and preplanning make the worst more bearable. Preplanning and practice are necessary to minimize fear, uncertainties, and errors.

7

Field Operations and Customer Relations

Product safety efforts do not end when the product is out the facility door. Some of the most valuable usage data will come from field service and customer service personnel. Therefore, the product safety professional must ensure that the lines of communication with these personnel are open and effective. This chapter discusses areas of concern to the product safety professional in the service, installation, repair, and maintenance operations and in post-sale communications with users. (See Chapter 4, Product Communications Design, for a discussion of other product communications.)

FIELD OPERATIONS

Field personnel (sales, service, installation, and technical) are the "eyes and ears" of an organization because they are in closest contact with the users. It is vital to have an open communication channel from users and customers back to the design and safety specialists (Figure 7–1). Some companies provide a toll-free number to monitor customer and user comments or complaints about the product. For such a channel to be used, field personnel first need to know how important it is to recognize problems and transmit what they see in the field to the shop or office. Both formal and informal communication systems are essential. In addition, a convenient method is needed that allows consumers and field personnel to inform the company about product functions, malfunctions, and near misses, accidents, misuses, and unexpected uses.

In short, field personnel should funnel data *from* users *to* the product department heads and the product safety professional within the company. These practices, and employees' awareness of them, should be monitored by the product safety professional. Some companies do periodic surveys of field personnel, customers, and/or dealers to extract usage data and to gauge customer satisfaction.

Figure 7-1.

This sample machine checklist can be used to record and communicate safety conditions from field service personnel to customers and to the product safety professional.

MACHINE CHECKLIST

Date: _____

Check one (✓):   ( ) Pre-Shipment   ( ) Machine Start-Up   ( ) Service Call

This is a Plastics Machinery Division requirement and must be completed by our technician.

Machine Model/Serial Number _____ Hours: _____

Customer: _____ Contact Person _____

Key: X = Satisfactory   O = Unsatisfactory   N = Not Applicable

Extruder

- ☐ Barrel shroud complete and intact
- ☐ Safety signs in place and readable
- ☐ Drive belt access guarded
- ☐ Hydraulic compartment door intact
- ☐ Electrical junction box covers closed and secured

- ☐ Electrical panel doors closed and interlocked
- ☐ Clutch compartment door intact
- ☐ Clutch compartment rear guard intact
- ☐ Air manifold exhaust muffler/central exhaust system installed

Clamp

- ☐ Operator safety doors intact
- ☐ Safety signs in place and readable
- ☐ Electrical interlocks deactivate hydraulic solenoid (hardware)
- ☐ Electrical interlocks deactivate hydraulic solenoid (software, where applicable)
- ☐ Pneumatic interlock blocks hydraulic plot
- ☐ Pneumatic interlock deactivates hydraulic solenoid by opening pressure switch

- ☐ Guards over platen in place and secured
- ☐ Stripper plate in place or alternate guarding used
- ☐ Front access step installed (where applicable)
- ☐ Guards for front clamp in place (where applicable)
- ☐ Low pressure close set to minimum practical operating pressure
- ☐ Controls functional (example emergency stop)

Swinging Arms

- ☐ Rotac pressure set to minimum practical operating pressure (arm can be stopped by worker)

- ☐ Electric eye intact and deactivates hydraulic solenoid

Cooling Conveyor/Serial Number _____

- ☐ Chain guards intact
- ☐ Clutch tension set to a minimum practical operating tension (rods can be stopped by worker)
- ☐ Plate adjacent to power roller set to 1/8" clearance (maximum)

- ☐ Leg clamps tight
- ☐ Crossover bridge in place (where applicable)
- ☐ Safety signs in place and readable
- ☐ Controls functional (example emergency stop)

Trimmer/Model Number _____   **Serial Number** _____

- ☐ Operator safety doors intact
- ☐ Safety interlocks operational
- ☐ Fixed inlet and outlet guards intact
- ☐ Motor belt guard intact
- ☐ Chain guards intact
- ☐ Safety signs in place and readable

- ☐ Bucket guard on in-feed and intact
- ☐ Bucket guard on exit and intact
- ☐ Electrical panel door closed and interlocked
- ☐ Controls functional (example emergency stop)
- ☐ Pusher jam limit switch operational (where applicable)

Airveyor

- ☐ Blower inlet guard intact

- ☐ Duct baffles (2) in place

Comments or Special Options _____
_____
_____

_____   _____
Signed for Manufacturer's Representative   Signed for Customer

Important Information on Reverse Side

Service

Most companies provide service functions to their customers, either directly or through the dealer or distributor or by use of subcontractors to fulfill servicing contracts. When there is a field service function, the product liability exposure may be significantly increased because the company may have extended its exposure beyond the confines of its manufacturing facility. At the same time, however, the company has a greater ability to influence how the product is used and can help control risks to users.

The product safety professional should carefully evaluate the service department procedures. The professional needs to assess not only the adequacy of these procedures and their contributions to product safety activities, but also the efficiency of the service department's product information feedback system.

In many companies, depending upon the type of product, service department personnel maintain close contact with customers. As a result, more than any other employees, service personnel are the most familiar with the customers and are usually the first to hear about customer complaints, accidents, reactions, and compliments regarding company products. They see product misuses and usually have some knowledge of incidents and accidents that have occurred. Many companies install computer systems to facilitate analysis of the data obtained from customers.

In view of the unique position of the service department, the company should attempt to get the greatest product safety benefits possible from this department by requiring their personnel to:

1. Use a check-off or report form when making a field service call to determine if the product and safety devices are in good operating condition and are being used properly. Service representatives should enter in the report the serial number, date serviced, reason for service, and specific service provided. When applicable, the company service representative should include all facts concerning any unsafe conditions observed, being careful not to express conclusions or opinions. The source of any opinions or conclusions by others, including the

customer, must be clearly identified if included in the report, to avoid the inference that they are opinions of the company representative. Also, any recommendations made to the customer to correct unsafe practices and conditions should be written into the report.

2. Ask the customer to sign the report form. A copy of the report should be given to the customer's contact person and the original retained in the service file. A report of this type will prove useful in the event of an accident at a later date and any subsequent claims involving the serviced product.

3. Refer customer complaints to a designated person who will then route them to the engineering, design, quality control, or other appropriate departments. Of course, safety-related complaints and reports of safety-related product incidents and accidents should be routed to the product safety professional, who can initiate further investigation, if necessary. Because of their closeness to users, field service personnel sometimes participate in safety reviews on new product designs or serve on the product safety committee, if one exists.

4. Formally review all service contracts, if any, to make sure that they are realistic with respect to the company's ability to comply with all provisions. Review also to ensure that any safety-related work is not overstated regarding its efficacy or thoroughness.

In some cases, a company does not service its products directly but subcontracts its service work to local contractors or uses its dealers to provide service. For these situations, the product safety professional should participate in evaluating (1) the selected subcontractors' knowledge of and ability to service the company products; (2) the service training for subcontractors, dealers, or distributors, if provided; and, (3) whether the company service instructions will provide sufficient guidance, in lieu of formal training, to anyone providing service for its products. In addition to ensuring that any contractor is properly qualified, it is also very important for the company to secure certificates of all appropriate insurance coverages.

Installation

The company is responsible for informing its customers about the safe use, maintenance, service, installation, and other applications of its products. If a product is meant to be installed by the customer, the installation instruction manual must be prepared in a language that the typical customer will understand. If the customer is not meant to perform the installation work but is likely to do so anyway, the customer must be warned in no uncertain terms of the hazards and consequences of improper installation.

In general, the installation manual should cover at least the following topics, as applicable:

- Electrical and other utility connections

- Location of the equipment within the work area

- Unpacking instructions

- Procedures for safe handling

- Safe assembly procedures

- Warnings

- Assembly diagrams

- Initial start-up procedures

- Gross weight

- Lifting points

- Prestart-up tests

- Specifications of items not furnished by the manufacturer but necessary for proper and safe installation (e.g., anchor bolts, brackets, fuses)

- Applicable codes

Required warnings in the installation instructions should be conspicuous and complete to better inform the user. If adequate instructions have not been provided, the company may be held liable for injuries resulting from the installation of its products. The safety professional should review installation agreements to ensure that they are realistic in terms of the company's ability to fulfill them.

Repair

The repair function is often overlooked as a source of potential safety problems. Consequently, the product safety professional must consider the following in any evaluation:

- Does the company repair its own products and others? If so, the company has considerably increased its product liability exposure. This is particularly true when repairing the products of others, because it may be accepting the product liability exposure of the other manufacturer as a function of the type and quality of repair performed.

- Where does the company perform its repair work—in its own shop or at the customer's location?

- Does the company use its dealers/distributors to repair its products? If so, are dealers/distributors adequately trained, either by the company or by virtue of experience, to perform repairs satisfactorily?

- Does the company prepare and retain detailed repair records?

- Does the company provide a repair warranty? If so, it should be examined to determine whether it is realistic and what, if any, liability the company has incurred from it in the past.

CUSTOMER RELATIONS

A product provider communicates with the customer/user long after the point of sale through manuals it provides with the product and through its reports and information bulletins on product changes that can improve user safety. The product safety professional should be involved in creating and reviewing such communications and in dealing with customer complaints, comments, and requests.

Handling Customer Complaints

Staff should not ignore a complaint or simply replace a defective product without notifying the product safety professional. The most insignificant incident might result in a liability claim or lawsuit later on. The product safety professional should coordinate all complaint-handling activities. These activities should be clearly spelled out so that customers, dealers, and field sales and service personnel know exactly how to report product malfunctions and product misuses to the company service department. The service department, in turn, must forward all complaints to the product safety professional. A company's quick response to product failures or complaints indicates its concern for customer satisfaction. The following are examples of some of the procedures that should be followed when a complaint is made:

- Visit the client and review the product problem on location, if possible.

- Attempt to retrieve the malfunctioning or damaged product, if possible.

- Review all records concerning the product's development, sales, and delivery.

- Conduct a thorough investigation into the cause of the accident, if possible.

- Obtain a copy of any accident reports, OSHA investigation reports, and so on.

Maintenance

Instructions pertaining to maintenance, installation, assembly, operation, service, trouble-shooting, and parts should be developed carefully. The maintenance instructions should clearly describe procedures for reducing wear and tear on the product and should indicate how often parts should be inspected, serviced, or replaced. It should cite the product limitations, warn of hazards that may be encountered during disassembly and maintenance, and emphasize the danger of not following the procedures printed in the manual. The consequences of product misuse or failure to maintain the product should be stressed.

To guard against misstatements regarding function, use, maintenance, installation, and the like, the company should have all of its communications reviewed by its product safety professional and appropriate product line personnel before they are published.

As in the case of service, installation, and repair, if the company uses subcontractors, dealers, or distributors to provide product maintenance and/or service to its customers, it must evaluate their knowledge and skills to provide this service. In addition, the company's maintenance contracts, if they are provided, should be reviewed to be sure the company can fulfill their provisions. As with service, installation, and repair subcontractors, the company should secure all appropriate certificates of insurance before using the contractor.

Reports and Information Bulletins

A company does not stop learning about ways to improve its products once they leave the facility. When a firm learns about or develops a product enhancement that can improve user safety, it should consider whether the improvement is significant enough to warrant a special effort to inform users of older products. Part of this decision will hinge on the feasibility of reaching the users. The product safety professional may or may not initiate communications with users but should ensure that the question is properly considered when an advance in user safety is made.

Users can be notified through one or more of the following media:

- Bulletins or letters about recently discovered product safety problems and how to avoid them or about newly found uses of products, when those uses are believed to be unsafe

- Retrofit guarding notices

- New standards or codes relevant to users

- Updated manuals when they have additional safety information

- Press releases to industry periodicals

- Additional warning signs

- Selling training to customers for their employees

- Newsletter to users of particular products

- Video cassettes, posters, booklets

- Field personnel

Field service personnel who work closely with users may be in the best position to convey certain types of information, such as unsafe practices observed; unsafe conditions observed; availability of new guards; safety devices; new literature; applying new safety signs to older machines; and, safety assessments with service reports. Not all field service personnel will become safety experts, and no one can guarantee the safety of a product by mere observation. Nevertheless, outstanding safety deficiencies and violations must be brought to the user's attention promptly, either in writing or verbally with confirmation in writing. Although field personnel cannot always reach the user, they generally have the best opportunity. Many companies use certified mail to augment field personnel reports. It is important that some form of written documentation is recorded for future reference and retrieval (Figures 7–2 and 7–3).

Figure 7–2.

A sample accident/injury report form to record customer reports and resolution by service representative.

ABC COMPANY

ACCIDENT/INJURY FORMS

Date of Call: __10/22/95__   Rep's Name: __W. PHONE__

Customer Name: __J. EASY SOFT TOUCH INC.__

Address: __6789 LEXINGTON AVE.__

           __ANYWHERE, USA__

Reason for Call: (Please give detailed description of the incident or comment as provided by the customer.)

__Customer reported that the printer sheet feed was still spinning__
__after opening the cover. Customer skinned knuckle on feed roll__

__when clearing jam.__

Resolution by Rep: (Please give detailed description of any final resolution you made with the customer.)

__Customer was told that the feed roll should not be rotating after__
__cover is opened. There must be an interlock malfunction.__ **Do not**

operate printer until fixed.__ Field Service has been notified and__
__respond within 24 hours.__

Referred To:
        Medical Dept.
        Insurance Dept.
        Product Manager
        Field Service
        Copy: Customer Service Supervisor/Corporate Insurance

Figure 7–3.
This is a computer printout of a service work order that resulted in an equipment design modification which pinned the switch and repositioned the actuator. Field Service initiated a program to retrofit the cover assembly at all customer facilities.

```
                        ABC COMPANY

Service Work Order     A1023      On Hold?   Yes      No

Entered: 10/23/95  By: W. Phone        Printed By:
Model No. 95M106       Priority:   10      COD:      No
Serial No. 123456      Type:      Safety   Status:   Closed
Description Printer
Product Ref.
Caller J. Easy
WO Phone 123-456-7890  Revision:  1.5.8    Retrofit:
Install Date 5/1/95    Equipment Status:   Division: 23
Cust. P.O.             W.O. Classification: Action By: Srv. Grp.
Serv. Cont.            Cust. Warrantee   1 Year
  Eff. Date:           Warrantee Effective: 6/1/95  -  5/31/96
  Bill Type: 2      Territory:

Customer: Soft Touch Inc.   Cust. System:   321
  Customer Address:              Equipment Address:

Lexington Area Service Center          same
6789 Lexington Ave.
Anywhere, U.S.A.

Customer Hours:       Open:      08:00      Close:  17:00

Problem Description:
Problem: FNJM                  Other/Unknown:

Cause Description:
Cause:  MSW

Repair Description:
Repair:   HREP                 Repaired Cover Assembly

Follow-up Call:
This W.O. was opened to follow-up on an injury that occurred to
the customer while clearing a jam. J. Fix was dispatched to review
incident #9876543. He found that the customer was closing the
cover very gently. The run switch was being activated yet the
latches were not engaged. He moved the switch down so that it
would not be engaged until the cover was fully latched. The cover
will not open now unless it is requested through the panel.

Distribution List:
Customer Service, Field Service, Manufacturing, Product Safety,
Product Design
```

8

Record Retention Requirements

Records are the backbone of a product and quality assurance program because they reflect the history of the product. Companies maintain records for three principal reasons: (1) to assist in identifying hazards, causes, or remedies necessary for design safety, redesign under recall procedures, remanufacture, or retrofit; (2) to retain experience data useful in future designs; and (3) to use in the defense of product liability claims. Good records indicate that the company's quality control system is functioning as planned, verify that a product was inspected, and often provide the actual inspection findings. (See also Chapter 10, Risk Management.)

The product safety coordinator should verify that there is a company-wide policy on what records to keep and for what period of time. A planned, periodic file review system should be part of that policy. Some additional reasons for retaining records are:

1. To establish the care taken to produce and sell a safe, reliable product

2. To demonstrate dedication on the part of company management to market a quality product

3. To comply with federal regulations covering design, manufacture, and sale of the company's products

4. To facilitate tracking the product and/or customer

5. To establish a sound data base of the design of old products that continue to be used

All of these reasons tend to document the fact that a company is genuinely concerned about the quality of its products and about the safety of those who use them.

COSTS AND BENEFITS

There are costs in terms of time and space as well as money associated with keeping records. For example, if the products are not consumable goods, such as food, drugs, and chemicals, it is simply not feasible from a practical standpoint to keep every quality control record or every internal memo having to do with the design of the products. For durable goods, the company must decide whether the value of certain documents truly outweighs the cost of retaining them. In general, the value of records and the storage costs vary from one situation to the next, so it is impossible to generalize about what records to keep and for how long. The remainder of this chapter contains suggestions for an ideal situation in which time, space, and money are not major impediments. These guidelines must be interpreted in light of each particular "real-world" situation.

WHICH RECORDS TO KEEP

Comprehensive records permit a company to readily identify and trace products that may have reached the customer in a defective or damaged condition. Having complete records can greatly assist a product recall or field-modification program.

In today's product liability environment, a company must not only manufacture and market quality products, but must also be able to defend against claims of product defect if the need arises. As a rule, companies should retain records that document a product's quality or safety from the purchase of raw materials through the manufacture, marketing, and distribution of the finished products.

Records that should be valuable to the product safety program include the following:

- Product design tests
- Product quality tests
- Samples of product batches
- Official notices of major design/safety importance
- Product drawings, specifications, warnings, packaging
- Manufacturing process specifications
- Material specifications
- Engineering changes, process changes

- Date coding

- Product line standards (i.e., ANSI, ASTM, and/or UL, and others)

- Purchase orders/sales contracts

- Order acknowledgments

- Vendor insurance agreements

- Educational materials

- Advertising/marketing literature, ads, articles, and others

- Catalogs

- Warranties

FEDERAL REGULATIONS

A company should be aware of federal regulations that affect record-keeping requirements. (Figure 8–1.) Some of the important federal safety regulations that a company must consider in the development of a record-keeping system are:

- Consumer Product Safety Act (PL 92–573)

- Federal Hazardous Substances Act (15 USC 1261)

- Federal Food, Drug and Cosmetic Act (21 USC 321)

- Poison Prevention Packaging Act (PL 91–601)

- Occupational Safety and Health Act (PL 91–596)

- Child Protection and Toy Act (PL 91–113)

- Magnuson-Moss Warranty—Federal Trade Commission

- Improvement Act (PL–93–637)

The requirements for maintaining financial records promulgated by the U.S. Internal Revenue Service are the largest set of such regulations in existence. Although the purpose of these IRS regulations is not safety related, nevertheless, there is considerable overlap between IRS requirements and good safety record-keeping practices. The IRS requirements serve as a mandatory baseline to which safety record-keeping requirements and needs can be added.

Figure 8–1.   Identification Data Required by the CPSC.

Information Required	Organization Responsible
Name, address of person notifying Commission	Manufacturer, distributor, retailer
Identification, description, price of product; name, address of the manufacturer; location of plants	Manufacturer, distributor, retailer, to the extent known to each
Nature of potential hazard	Manufacturer, distributor, retailer
Date of receipt of data supporting conclusion that potential product hazard existed	Manufacturer, distributor, retailer
Type of supporting data (i.e., complaints, testing); if consumer complaints, copies should be forwarded to the CPSC	Manufacturer, distributor, retailer
Nature of potential injury	Manufacturer, distributor, retailer
Number, nature, and severity of injuries that have occurred, if any	Manufacturer, distributor, retailer to the extent known to each
Number of products that present a potential hazard and number of units of each product	Manufacturer; distributor/retailer only to extent known from products at hand
Number of units of each product in the hands consumers	Manufacturer; distributor/retailer only to extent known from products at hand
Manufacturing and shipping dates for each unit	Manufacturer, distributor/retailer only to extent known
Distribution points and dates and number of units distributed	Manufacturer, distributor
Product model numbers, serial numbers, or identifying marks, as appropriate	Manufacturer, distributor, retailer
Location on product of model number, serial number, or identifying mark, as appropriate	Manufacturer, distributor, retailer
Whether manufacture of the product has ceased	Manufacturer

Figure 8–1.   Identification Data Required by the CPSC. Continued

Completed, in process, or planned corrective action and time involved	Manufacturer
Planned engineering changes to comply with an applicable consumer product safety rule and timetable for changes	Manufacturer
Description of in-factory tests to comply and/or failure to comply with an applicable consumer product safety rule	Manufacturer
New quality controls initiated to avoid the product hazard and/or the failure to comply with an applicable consumer product safety rule; timetable for changes	Manufacturer
Past, present, or future advice about product to purchasers and to distributor, retailer, consumers; method of advice	Manufacturer, distributor, retailer
Whether public notice of the defect or failure to comply has been or will be given. If given, furnish copy to the Commission.	Manufacturer, distributor, retailer
Past, present, or future refund, replacement, or repair actions	Manufacturer, distributor, retailer
Whether notice has been or will be mailed to each manufacturer, distributor, or retailer of such product	Manufacturer, distributor, retailer
What effort has been or will be made to notify consumers directly where such consumers are known	Manufacturer, distributor, retailer
Plans for the proposed disposition of finished goods and work-in-process inventory	Manufacturer

As a rule of thumb, if an organization's products are regulated, it should have a record-keeping system comprehensive enough to be able to implement whatever remedial action required by either the organization or a federal regulatory agency. Preferably, the organization should be able to retrieve a list of previous owners, operators, holders, and so on in case recall notification is necessary. For example, if the Consumer Product Safety Commission judges a product to be hazardous, a company may be ordered to provide public notice of the hazard. In addition, the company may be ordered to take remedial action, such as repair, modification, or replacement, and in extreme cases, conduct a complete product recall.

INTERNAL REQUIREMENTS

A company must maintain records of pertinent information related to the design, manufacture, marketing, testing and sales of products that pose some accident risk. Of particular value are those records that document design decisions. A manufacturer should be able to show that important development decisions were made affecting design, materials chosen, and safety. Also, records of why a certain production technique was chosen, such as the choice between forged and cast, should be retained. Records can also document the testing to which a product was subjected and the reasons for product modifications and improvements. When a significant hazard cannot be eliminated, the records should show conclusively why it could not be done.

RECORD RETENTION SCHEDULES

When establishing a retention schedule for records of tests, analyses, quality control procedures, lot numbers, serial numbers, and shipping procedures, a company should take into consideration the life of the product plus a period to account for factors such as statutes of limitation. Generally speaking, if a company cannot accurately define the "life" of its product, it should consider retaining all product safety records in perpetuity. If this decision creates record storage or maintenance difficulties, the company can use microfilm, computer information storage, or a record compilation system. The product safety coordinator must make sure that key personnel fully understand why records are being maintained, what they contain, and how long they should be retained.

Items for the product safety professional to consider:

- Completeness of engineering records

- Availability of discontinued as well as of current quality control manuals

- For high-volume products, photographs of major installations to back up the engineering records

- Accident and complaint records

- Sales and change records going back for at least the life of the product

- Design changes

- Minutes of design review meetings

FORMAT OF RECORDS

The coordinator should review the language used to refer to product changes in company forms, reports, and memos. The review could be done in consultation with the company lawyer to evaluate possible interpretations of the wording of such forms.

In the course of product liability cases, both sides can effectively use the "discovery" process. The plaintiff's lawyer invariably searches the defendant's records for evidence. The defendant's lawyer will collect all evidence of the accident and request company records to substantiate inconsistencies in the alleged chain of causation. (See Chapter 10, Risk Management, for more information on legal and insurance issues.) A manufacturer's records may substantially affect the outcome of a product liability case.

9 Recall Preparedness

No organization wants to issue a product recall or field modification, yet many companies must plan for this contingency. A *mandatory* recall or field modification can develop for any company manufacturing or distributing products under the purview of the Consumer Product Safety Commission (CPSC), that is, for most consumer products manufacturers. Other companies may encounter situations in which a *voluntary* recall or field modification becomes warranted. By establishing a recall policy and allocating funds and personnel before a crisis, the company can more adequately protect the product users and the corporation. (See Appendix 4, CPSC Recall Handbook.) Top management should give staff and line personnel the objectives and guidelines they need to reduce potential confusion and costly mishandling in a recall situation.

The purposes of an established recall policy include:

1. Protecting the customer/user

2. Removing unacceptable or questionable products from the market at the least cost and inconvenience to the user

3. Complying with all applicable laws and regulations

4. Protecting the assets of the corporation

PRODUCT IDENTIFICATION AND TRACKING

Product users are not a static group. Some companies try to keep track of their product users by compiling sales records of parts. All field operating personnel, dealers, and distributors should have clear, comprehensive guidelines about what to do if an accident is reported. Their conformance to these operating requirements should be part of the criteria by which the dealers are qualified to distribute the product of the manufacturer.

For most consumer products, the decision to alert users about some aspect of safety is regulated by the CPSC. To be prepared for a potential recall, the CPSC requires that certain identification data be kept by the manufacturer, distributor, and/or retailer. (See Figure 8–1 for CPSC requirements and the organization responsible for retaining the data.)

A product recall or field modification may become a reality for almost any manufacturer and may involve those who supply components parts, materials, and services for those products. Therefore, the product safety professional must be prepared to evaluate the company to determine whether it is capable of implementing a successful product recall or field-modification program should one become necessary.

In addition, recall or field modification should be considered in those cases where the company is aware of or has itself developed an "improvement" to its product (e.g., a guard or shield). In some cases, the improvement may have been developed after the sale of earlier product models and, technically, could and should have been incorporated into subsequent models. The company must be prepared to advise its customers of the available product improvement, the hazard it eliminates, and what they must do to incorporate it into their current product models.

If the company discovers that substantial performance or safety problems exist in some or all products that have already been shipped, it may be required to recall or field-modify these products. The closer the company can come to identifying the offending production cycle or segment, the less it will cost to correct the problem. Instead of requiring a full day of production, the correction may take only one hour or one operation.

The identification of the specific lots, batches, quantities, or units of the product to be recalled or modified in the field can be a difficult procedure unless a system of adequate tracking has been established during the product planning and manufacturing stages. High-cost products, custom-designed products, and the like are usually traceable to the individual purchaser and sometimes to subsequent owners. For high-volume "shelf items" of modest cost, such tracking is not usually practical, and other means of limiting the extent of potential recalls should be considered.

If a firm must conduct a product recall or field-modification program, the quantity of product that must be recalled or modified and the cost to do so can be minimized if the firm can pinpoint the exact number of defective products, parts, or components involved. Where practical, products should be marked in some way, even though the means of marking a product so that the identification survives use is sometimes difficult, if not impossible. However, no code, date, serial number, or other marking will be useful unless the company can identify which batches, materials, components, processes, and so on were responsible for the suspect products. Therefore, a continuous log of all batches, materials, processes, and product changes should be maintained. This log must be sufficiently detailed to permit correlation with the product marking or identification system.

The benefit of having a good product information retrieval system is, generally, reduced product recall or field modification. Other advantages include greater ease in furnishing replacement parts to customers and service centers and the ability to correlate product returns, complaints, and field experience records with changes in product design, production, and quality control procedures. In addition, the CPSC has clearly indicated that if a company's records do not enable it to recall or modify its products effectively, the CPSC may issue a notice to the news media advising the public of the potential hazard. Thus, a system which permits the quick recall or field modification of products is an obvious economic advantage to a company.

FIELD INFORMATION SYSTEM

A company must receive feedback from the field about the performance of its products. The product safety professional should determine the effectiveness of the field information system in providing data about the type of product and the product distribution system involved. The coordinator should thoroughly evaluate the system's ability (1) to identify and track a product from the raw material through final sales and distribution stages; (2) to acquire and use field data (complaints, incidents, and accidents); and (3) to implement product field-modification or recall action, where appropriate.

DATA COLLECTION

Products that potentially may be recalled for safety reasons or may require safety bulletins to be issued should have record-keeping systems set up *in advance* to locate as many users as possible. (See Chapter 8, Record Retention Requirements.)

Purchasers of high-cost, low-volume items are far easier to reach than those of low-cost, high-volume items. For example, a serial-numbered machine tool is much more likely to have a known user than is a can opener. Nevertheless, the product safety professional should ensure that all feasible records are retained and compiled to maximize the effectiveness of any recall. For some products this may entail looking into the record retention policies of wholesalers, distributors, and others in the sales channels. Sources of user data include warranty cards, coupon returns, and parts sales. High-cost product manufacturers also have purchase orders and sales contracts. Manufacturers should consider recall possibilities when deciding whether to put serial numbers on their product.

For chemical and food products made in batches, many producers keep batch samples for the expected life of the product. By resolving questions or complaints, such samples can help eliminate the need for a recall.

ANALYSIS OF DATA

A reasonably detailed report used with a data collection and analysis system should enable a company to evaluate accurately each complaint, incident, and accident report received and to assess any developing problem. The product safety professional should be advised of all complaints having safety implications and of significant trends. He or she should also be able to verify, through company records, the results of any field data analysis and what corrective action, if any, was taken.

Because manufactured products are so diverse, no specific data collection and analysis system is applicable to all companies. However, every data-reporting system must provide the answers to the following questions:

1. *Who is the customer or user?* The customer's name and location, and where the product is being used, must appear on the product complaint form. A group of complaint records from customers sometimes reveals problems associated with specific products. Further investigation may determine that unusual environmental or customer application problems exist. A tabulation of complaint records by geographic area occasionally can pinpoint transportation, handling, or storage problems.

2. *What kind of product is involved?* A company must be able to specifically determine which product or product line is causing a problem. Space should be provided on the complaint report form for recording information such as:

- Model name

- Serial number

- Lot number

- Manufacturing date code

- Carton sequence number

- Contract number

The purposes of recording these data are (1) to permit tracing the approximate date of manufacture and the responsible operator; (2) to determine the pertinent engineering specifications; and (3) to associate the product with particular batches of raw materials or component parts. If sufficient data are provided, a company can analyze the information and determine what, if any, corrective action should be taken.

3. *What is the problem?* A company must obtain a complete description of the customer's problem if it is to take meaningful corrective action. The company must be able to determine if a malfunction occurred or if the appearance of the product rendered it unfit for service. A completed complaint report form should include answers to the following questions:

- What was the specific nature of the complaint?

- Was the product installed properly?

- Were operating and installation instructions furnished? Followed?

- Were all the necessary parts received?

- Was the appearance of the product satisfactory when first received?

- Was the performance of the product initially satisfactory?

- Was the appearance of the product satisfactory after a period of operation?

- Did discoloration or other deteriorations in appearance or performance become evident with the lapse of time?

A company should also be interested in obtaining data pertaining to the efficiency of the product packaging, transportation, and handling systems., particularly if the complaint may have resulted from product damage incurred in transit.

4. *How is the product being used?* The company must consider the potential uses and misuses of a product when it is being designed. Sometimes, however, a customer subjects the product to conditions that were not anticipated by the designers. It is important, therefore, that as much detail as is practical be reported on the customer's use of the product.

RECALL OR FIELD-MODIFICATION PLAN

The following product recall or field-modification plan outlines the general procedures a company should consider. Each company's needs will, of course, be different and must be defined by the product safety professional after evaluating the record-keeping and product-tracking systems.

Based on information acquired from complaints, incidents, and accident reports from customers, distributors, dealers, or internal testing or evaluation, a company must be able to determine immediately if a substantial hazard exists. Techniques for making this determination include (1) on-site investigation and/or failure analysis of the product by the company or an independent laboratory; (2) analyses of other units of the same product batch; and, (3) evaluation by in-house tests or other records.

If a substantial product hazard does exist, the following steps should be taken, as appropriate:

1. Stop production and distribution of the hazardous product.

2. Involve legal counsel in planning and conducting a product recall or field-modification program.

3. Determine the number or identity of the products to be recalled from the design, production, and quality control records.

4. Determine from sales and distribution records, the purchasers of the involved products and their geographical areas.

5. Assign responsibility for estimating the cost of the proposed product recall/field-modification to an appropriate individual/department.

6. Supply reports on the seriousness of the hazard, the number of units involved, and the estimated cost to recall or modify to the individual(s) responsible for actually making the recall or field-modification decision.

7. If the product comes under the Consumer Product Safety Act, have the above individual(s) notify the CPSC of any substantial hazard within the time limit required by CPSC regulations and coordinate all subsequent product recall or field-modification activities with the CPSC. (For products under the jurisdiction of other federal government agencies, i.e., drugs, foods, automobiles, and so on, the product hazard should be reported to the appropriate agency and the recall or field modification coordinated with that agency.)

8. Notify dealers and/or distributors of the safety problem and advise them that the product recall or field-modification program will commence on a certain date. Dealers and distributors must be given the proper procedures to be followed when the program commences (e.g., replacements of products, field modification of products). These procedures should also outline the reimbursement steps that will enable dealers to recover their costs for time, labor, and so on.

9. Initiate procedures to provide dealers and/or distributors with replacement products or parts for the recall or field-modification program.

10. Telephone major customers and define the problem and product recall or field-modification program steps.

11. Follow up by writing a product hazard letter to be sent to all customers. This letter must clearly identify the product involved, the hazard, and its estimated severity. The company should notify customers by telegram or by certified mail if the product hazard is estimated to be serious. The letter or telegram should clearly state the actions the customer should take, e.g., discontinue use immediately, take product to nearest dealer or distributor for refund, replacement, repair, and so on.

12. If necessary, develop newspaper, magazine, radio, and/or TV press releases identifying the product and the actions required. (See the Public Relations section in Chapter 6, Marketing and Sales Activities).

13. Send letters or telegrams to customers, distributors, and dealers announcing the product recall or field-modification program. If necessary, place advertisements in major newspapers and magazines and on major radio and TV stations announcing the recall or field-modification program.

14. Develop and retain records defining the effectiveness of the product recall or field-modification program. Sort records by dealer or distributor, and by city and geographical area. The company must follow up in those instances where no response has been received from customers.

15. Report results, as appropriate, to the CPSC and other federal regulatory agencies.

When a company's customer records are incomplete or nonexistent, it may be necessary to:

1. Determine the geographical areas where the affected products were sold.

2. Obtain the assistance of distributors, dealers, or retailer in reaching purchasers for notification of the recall.

3. Develop newspaper, magazine, radio, and TV advertisements for use in the appropriate geographical sales areas. (The purpose of these advertisements is to announce the product hazard, the planned product recall or field-modification program, and how to comply with the program.)

NOTIFICATION OF GOVERNMENT AGENCIES

Some government agencies require reports of any product-related accident data and user complaints. Some states, such as New Jersey, also require recall notification. The following is a partial listing of agencies that may affect the retailer, wholesaler, and importer. Check with the pertinent agency to verify reporting requirements and recall procedures for specific products:

- Consumer Product Safety Commission

- Federal Food and Drug Administration

- United States Environmental Protection Agency

- Federal Communications Commission

- United States Coast Guard

- National Highway Traffic Safety Agency

- Nuclear Regulatory Commission

10 Risk Management

It is commonly assumed that the risk management and legal departments of a company only have a post-accident role in managing a claim or lawsuit. However, these departments can help the rest of the organization reduce the frequency of claims and minimize their impact upon the company. For smaller organizations that do not have such departments, a knowledgeable attorney and the loss control or claim representative of an insurance carrier and/or broker can be valuable risk-management resources. The product safety professional should know the legal and insurance issues that affect product safety and how to ask for assistance from the specialists in these areas. (For more information, see Warren Freedman, *Product Liability for Corporate Counsels, Controllers, and Product Safety Executives*, New York: Van Nostrand Reinhold Company, 1984; Charles O. Smith, *Products Liability: Are You Vulnerable?* Englewood Cliffs, NJ: Prentice-Hall, Inc., 1981; and the latest edition of *Black's Law Dictionary*, St. Paul, MN: West Publishing Company.)

It is beyond the scope of this book to present legal case histories or to make the reader an expert in risk management. Because liability laws and their applications may vary from state to state and within various jurisdictions, the reader should consult with a specialist in the appropriate field before taking any action.

This chapter discusses the functions of the legal department or retained attorney, the legal basis for product liability suits, legal approaches, the functions of the risk management department or carrier, and what to do in the event of a complaint or litigation.

LEGAL SPECIALISTS

People often assume that a lawyer is an expert in product safety and product liability simply because he or she practices law. Actually, liability is a specialty area in which most practicing attorneys have only brief experience. When choosing legal counsel, companies should select lawyers who are experienced in tort law, in general, and in products liability law, in particular.

Advisory Functions

Legal specialists should act as advisors to the product safety professional and others involved in critical product safety matters within the company. As advisors, these specialists are responsible for informing the company's key management personnel about the effect upon the company of the following:

1. Current theories of negligence, strict liability, and warranty, and statutes and regulations applicable to the company's products;

2. Recent legal decisions and current legal trends affecting the company's products, including identifying product liability cases involving competitors; and,

3. Additional liability issues may arise if the company is engaged in the importing of parts, components, or products. If there is a product-related injury and the foreign supplier does not have a United States affiliation (i.e., a "legal presence"), the importer may lose the status of a middleman and have imposed the full legal responsibilities of the original manufacturer. Companies should try to get a certificate of product liability insurance coverage and a hold-harmless and indemnification agreement.

Too often, companies use their legal department or retained attorney only when product safety problems already exist or product liability litigation becomes imminent. Legal specialists should be involved in the day-to-day functions that promote product safety and liability prevention.

The legal specialist should oversee or review the following company documents for their contribution to the company's product safety program:

- Invoices, forms, purchase orders and purchase order acknowledgments, sales agreements, disclaimers, hold-harmless and indemnification agreements, warranties/guarantees, and any other product-related contracts or documents that could legally bind the company

- Record retention policies

- Vendor endorsements to product liability insurance policies

- Decisions and procedures for product recalls, retrofit, and product user safety notifications

- Warnings

- Advertising

- All product-related literature

The product safety professional should be able to evaluate the adequacy of the legal department's or outside counsel's contribution to the company product safety program, based upon the duties listed above. If the company has a risk manager, he or she also should be involved in this process. Legal counsel, inside or outside, should be experienced in product safety matters.

Coordination Functions

When a product claim or a lawsuit is presented, the legal specialist should manage the following activities:

- All product accident investigations, including working with the insurance carrier. (Depending upon the organization, this may be the responsibility of the insurance or risk management department.)

- All product claim defense matters from the retention of local counsel to settlement negotiations as well as recommendations of experts.

BASES FOR LAWSUITS

The product safety professional should know the legal bases for lawsuits to evaluate how the company's products may be at risk. The professional should also consult checklists and/or other surveys done by the risk management department. (See also Chapter 1, Basic Concepts, and the Glossary. See Smith, 1981; Freedman, 1984; Hursh & Bailey, 1974.)

The occurrence of a product-related injury is not, by itself, grounds for recovering damages. The plaintiff must prove that the manufacturer has breached some legal duty or that the product was defective. The liability of the manufacturer will be determined based upon one or more of several legal theories: (1) negligence; (2) breach of warranty (express or implied); (3) strict liability; and, (4) in certain jurisdictions, a deceptive trade practices act.

These theories of liability can vary in their application from one jurisdiction to the next and from case to case. For this reason, the product safety professional should consult the legal department or specialist regarding the law that applies to each specific case.

In negligence claims, the object of the plaintiff is to prove that the manufacturer failed to use reasonable care in designing, testing, manufacturing, or distributing the product. In a breach of warranty claim, the focus is upon the express or implied guarantees or representations made about the product.

In most states, a lawsuit may be based upon some form of strict liability. This theory of recovery focuses only on the product itself. Because it is not a fault-based theory, defenses of contributory or comparative negligence (improper use by the consumer or user) do not directly apply. The strict liability theory is based upon the premise that the manufacturer has the most information about the product, the most control of the design, and so on and is best able to distribute losses caused by injuries from using the product. There has been an expansion in types of evidence and proof allowed to show a defect in the product.

Defective Products

The product may be judged defective if it is found to be improperly designed, improperly manufactured, tested, marketed, and the like, or to have inadequate warnings or instructions. Product liability law is state law, and there are significant variations among states in the theories of recovery, permissible evidence, the amount of evidence necessary to find the product defective, and the possible defenses available to the company. The product safety professional as well as the engineers and managers need to become familiar with the basic laws or legal concepts that impinge on their products and operations.

Foreseeable Misuse

Because manufacturers/sellers are assumed to be experts in regard to their product, they are assumed to know the potential users, user environments, uses of the product, and any reasonably foreseeable misuses. For example, if it is foreseeable that a particularly burdensome guard may be removed by the user and thus cause injury, the manufacturer/seller is responsible for designing a more practical guard if feasible, or, otherwise, to warn against its removal. If it is reasonably foreseeable that the product will be used by functionally illiterate or non-English-speaking workers, it may be argued that the manufacturer should have used pictorial warnings instead of written words.

Punitive Damages

If the company has acted "willfully, wantonly, or with reckless disregard" in selling a product that is unreasonably dangerous, large punitive damage awards may be granted in addition to the compensatory award. The award of such damages is based on the manufacturer's (1) knowledge of the defect, (2) failure to take remedial action, and (3) corporate misconduct. The award may be many times the amount of the compensatory award, and generally is determined by the financial resources of the company and the extent to which the company's actions "shock the conscience of the court." (See Chapter 8, Record Retention Requirements, for information on the records a company should keep.)

Punitive damage awards are relatively rare, but their severity should give pause to any product safety professional who is tempted to sit idly by while safety is sacrificed for expediency.

Disclaimers and Hold-Harmless Agreements

Manufacturers/sellers often use disclaimers or hold-harmless clauses in product literature, contracts, or business forms in order to limit or redirect liabilities. These clauses, however, have certain legal limitations. Disclaimers of warranty may limit economic damages between buyers and sellers of goods, but they are often ineffective against claims for personal injury. Hold-harmless clauses are intended to fix, by contract, the liability between two parties to another third party. For example, Company A can require that vendors whose merchandise it sells must indemnify Company A from any claim made by a customer injured by its product. Such clauses are usually enforceable, but their application may be limited by law or by circumstances peculiar to individual situations. Furthermore, they may be unacceptable from a purely business standpoint.

Disclaimers must conform to statutes about the language used, the size of type used, and their location. If a company wants to exclude a warranty of merchantability, the disclaimer must be in larger type than surrounding language, and it must include the word "merchantability." For example,

The Company Disclaims All Implied Warranties of Merchantability

Or, to exclude the warranty of fitness for a particular purpose:

The Company Disclaims All Warranties of Fitness for a Particular Purpose

A company may also attempt to limit its liability for incidental or consequential damages, except for those relating to personal injuries:

The Company Shall In No Event Be Liable For Incidental or Consequential Damages, Including, Without Limitation, Lost Profits, Loss of Income, Loss of Business Opportunity, Loss of Use, and Other Related Expenses.

The use of the above clauses and others is commonly referred to as "the battle of the forms." Only the rudiments of this issue have been discussed here. The product safety professional, the risk manager, the legal department, and possibly others should review use of these disclaimers in much greater detail.

LEGAL APPROACHES

Soon after a claim becomes a lawsuit, the product manufacturer (the defendant) may find itself in a courtroom at a trial. In product liability trials, a company can use a defensive or offensive approach, or both approaches, depending on the circumstances of the case.

Defensive approaches often follow one of two plans. The first plan is to refute the plaintiff's theory or theories with facts. The typical plaintiff theories are that the product is defective or unreasonably dangerous, that the product was negligently designed or manufactured, or that it failed to meet its implied warranties of fitness of purpose or merchantability. To succeed by this approach, defendants must refute the factual basis of all plaintiff arguments or theories. Refuting that the product is defective may also involve discussing the pros and cons of the product in light of either risk/benefit analysis or the consumer expectations test. Very briefly, these legal theories evaluate whether product benefits outweigh the risks of harm and whether a product is more hazardous than the ordinary user contemplates.

The second principal defensive plan is to argue causation. That is, the company tries to show that whatever might have been the problem with a product, it was not the cause of the accident/injury that is the subject of the lawsuit.

The offensive approach is not necessarily to refute anything but rather to prove one of the common affirmative defenses: "assumption of the risk," "intervening superseding cause," "contributory negligence or misuse of the product," "state of the art," or, in rare cases, "collateral estoppel." Which of these affirmative defenses may be available varies from state to state.

Assumption of the risk is a defense in which the defendant must prove that the injury or property damage was the result of a hazard that (1) was obvious to the plaintiff, (2) was recognized and understood by him or her, and (3) was voluntarily accepted by him or her. For example, if a user removes the guard from a circular saw and uses it in spite of clear warnings or obvious danger, he has assumed the risk. In other words, the plaintiff voluntarily and unreasonably encountered a known risk.

This argument leads to counterarguments that the injured person did not realize the risks involved or the gravity of the possible injuries or that the injured person's behavior was prompted by his or her employer's instruction and based, in part, on habitual practice.

"Intervening superseding cause" is the legal term for the defense that someone did something to the product after it left the control of the defendant and that this action was the real cause of the accident rather than any action on the defendant's part. This defense is common when the injured person removes a safety feature, for example, or when a dealer or distributor assembles, modifies, or customizes a product.

This defense leads to a counterargument that whatever happened after the product left the manufacturer's control was foreseeable and reasonable. Knowing what was likely to happen, it might be argued, the manufacturer could have taken action, for example, equipped the product with a guard that is less likely to be removed, by-passed, or disengaged, and/or warned users against such practice. Plaintiffs also argue that guards should be equipped with interlock switches to disengage the machinery if the guard are removed.

Contributory negligence is a defense in which the defendant tries to prove that the plaintiff was at fault in the use of the product. That is, the plaintiff failed to use it as a reasonable person would under the circumstances, and that this use contributed to the injury. This defense is based on the old common law idea that a plaintiff should not recover damages if he or she contributed to the accident. If this is the applicable law in the jurisdiction, and the plaintiff who is found to have partially contributed to the accident would be unable to recover damages.

Contributory negligence can be used as a defense only in a case based on negligence; it is inapplicable in cases based on strict liability.

Contributory negligence has been discarded in most states and replaced by the legal concept of comparative negligence. Under this theory, the plaintiff's fault is compared to that of the defendant's. If the plaintiff's fault is less than that of the defendant's, the plaintiff may recover a proportionate share of the awarded damages. The formula for determining that share varies from one jurisdiction to another. In some states, if the plaintiff's fault exceeds 50%, the plaintiff will be barred from any recovery.

Although liability based on negligence is a separate cause of action from one based on strict liability, in many states strict liability has borrowed the "comparative negligence" concept from the law of negligence. The parallel concept under strict liability is "comparative fault." Under comparative fault, the court (usually the jury) distributes the fault for an injury among the parties before the court—the plaintiff or injured party, the manufacturer, the retailer, the employer, or other defendants. Generally, in comparative fault jurisdictions, the plaintiff is not allowed to recover if the jury finds the plaintiff more than 50% at fault. Lesser degrees of fault on the part of the plaintiff are treated differently among the respective states. In some states, the injured party must be less responsible for the injury than any single defendant to recover an award. The formula for the injured party's award varies with the jurisdiction and the specific circumstances.

In those states with "joint and several liability," it is possible for a defendant found to have only a small percentage of liability under comparative fault to be assessed the entire monetary award to the plaintiff. Such liabilities against defendant product manufacturers are most likely to occur with regard to industrial products used in the workplace. Workers' compensation statutes limit the liability of employers throughout the United States, making employers' liability in product cases limited or nonexistent. Thus, product manufacturers may be responsible for their own comparative fault and for that of the employer as well.

With product liability cases coming to trial that involve machines manufactured 10 to 40 years ago, the defense may wish to argue that manufacturing processes were "state of the art" at the time the machine was designed and manufactured. As discussed previously, "state of the art" is that level of relevant scientific and technological knowledge existing at the time the product was designed and/or manufactured. Unfortunately, some courts do not accept "state of the art" as a defense in strict liability cases because neither the manufacturer's exercise of due care nor negligence is relevant. In these courts, state-of-the-art evidence is accepted only when a product is considered unsafe. It may be argued that courts which prohibit use of state-of-the-art evidence in strict liability cases are blurring the distinction between strict liability and absolute liability.

"Collateral estoppel" is a legal doctrine that can be used as an affirmative defense, but it is often more useful to the plaintiff than to the defendant. Collateral estoppel means that a party to a lawsuit is estopped (prohibited) from arguing the case on liability. The estopped party automatically loses on the issue of liability. If the estopped party is the defendant, the sole question for the court to consider is the amount of damages.

In a product liability case, collateral estoppel can be invoked when a finding was made in a previous lawsuit involving the same product and the same accident circumstances. By collateral estoppel, both plaintiff and defendant in a lawsuit are subject to the findings of a previous trial, so the same case does not have to be tried repeatedly.

Collateral estoppel is infrequently invoked, relatively speaking. This is so because in the absence of overwhelming, incontrovertible evidence to the contrary, courts tend to accept arguments that the previously litigated product was not exactly the same or that the previous accident or circumstances were not identical.

RISK MANAGEMENT DEPARTMENT

Too often, a company's insurance or risk management department is viewed as merely the department that buys insurance and reports claims to the insurance carrier. In fact, the insurance or risk management department may have valuable knowledge and experience that the product safety professional should use in developing product safety programs.

The department responsible for handling product liability claims will vary, depending upon the size and structure of the company and the type of product it manufactures. Small organizations that have no risk management department may rely upon the services of their insurance agent or broker and/or insurance carrier. The product safety department is often responsible for investigation and analysis of product safety incidents. (McGuire, 1979)

Because of its knowledge of past accidents, claims-handling procedures, policy provisions, and limits, the risk management department should participate with the safety professional in analyzing potential product liability exposure from existing and new products and from the products of recently acquired or to-be-acquired companies. Commercially available risk management checklists are valuable in this process.

Insurance Carriers and Accident Investigation

This section discusses the services of the risk management department and insurance carrier, and the procedures to follow when an accident becomes a claim.

Although many large companies refer to themselves as "self-insured," this is rarely completely accurate. They may have a "deductible" or "self-insured retention" of many thousands, perhaps even millions of dollars. However, some form of excess or umbrella insurance is usually purchased as protection against claims so large that they might destroy or seriously threaten the continued existence of the company.

Most insurance carriers maintain a keen interest in the prevention of serious injury to customers of their insureds. This interest is reflected in the resources, such as loss control departments, within insurance companies devoted to helping insureds minimize loss through claims.

Manufacturers should contact their broker or underwriter to explore the product safety resources available within the loss control department of their insurance company.

The initial investigation of a product safety incident is usually conducted by, or in cooperation with, the manufacturer or seller, who is most familiar with the product involved. This information should be promptly reported internally, as appropriate. If required by the insurance contract, the information should also be reported to the insurance carrier. The insurance carrier can help the product safety professional and company management prepare cost studies that define the impact of product safety problems on the financial health of the corporation. The carrier also can help develop a cost-allocation system so that financial responsibility for claim costs can be passed along to the proper department or division within the company to encourage each department's product safety efforts.

Although the manufacturer/seller is the expert on the products being produced, the insurance representative frequently can provide helpful advice on product injuries based on the experience of similar operations in other industries. The product safety professional should inquire whether the insurance carrier has a product safety specialist who can supply an independent point of view that may help the management team put its accident investigation in clearer perspective.

Handling a Complaint or Claim

When complaints arise, involved personnel should obtain as much information as they can right away, and, if possible, secure the damaged or broken part. There probably will be no better opportunity to obtain the information and/or evidence than soon after an accident or complaint. All data should be factual. Because inexperienced investigators may make mistakes while gathering data, they should avoid drawing conclusions in accident or incident reports. All field, switchboard, mailroom, distributor, and service personnel should be instructed to forward all claim notifications, legal papers, photographs, and/or accident reports to the product safety professional, or to the appropriate designee, by the quickest means available (fax, telegram, overnight mail).

Depending on the circumstances, the product safety professional or legal department may appoint a claims coordinator to coordinate activities between and within the legal department, and between the product safety personnel and the insurance carrier. Among other things, the coordinator should keep track of legal deadlines for filing notices and motions, and discovery deadlines; gather relevant internal records; and so on. If a company fails to respond within the prescribed time period, it risks having a default judgment imposed on it. The claims coordinator should start a case file. Preliminary information to be collected includes the type and extent of injuries; damage; names of persons involved; and when, where, and the reasons why the accident occurred. A form should be used to ensure that all information is consistently gathered (Figure 10–1). Notes should be signed and dated.

The claims coordinator should also be sure that all inquiries and notifications are properly routed, coordinate the investigation, maintain liaison with local counsel and the insurance carrier, gather further information, and perform other duties as required.

From a product liability viewpoint, the following details about the extent of the injuries or damage should be obtained:

- State of injured person's health before the injury

- Severity, extent, and effects of injuries sustained

- Current and projected future cost of medical and hospital care

- Length of hospital and home confinement

- Nature of treatments and persons administering

- Any permanent disfigurement

- Loss of earnings, profits, services, or impairment of future earning capacity

- Extent and cost of rehabilitation

Figure 10–1.
An incident/accident investigation report form helps ensure that all relevant details are obtained and documented.

Liability: The Legal and Insurance Departments

PRODUCT INCIDENT/ACCIDENT INVESTIGATION REPORT

PRODUCT NAME _____

CUSTOMER'S NAME AND ADDRESS

(MODEL NO.)   (SERIAL NO.)   (LOT NO.)

REPORTED LOCATION OF INCIDENT/ACCIDENT

DATE OF INCIDENT/ACCIDENT   TIME   AM   PM   DATE REPORTED

PERSONAL INJURY	PROPERTY DAMAGE
NAME AND ADDRESS OF INJURED PERSON	PROPERTY DAMAGED _____
	NATURE OF DAMAGE _____
OCCUPATION _____ AGE _____	
NATURE OF INJURY _____	EXTENT OF DAMAGE _____
PART OF BODY INJURED _____	

WITNESSES: NAMES AND ADDRESSES
(1) _____
(2) _____
(3) _____
(4) _____
(5) _____

DESCRIBE THE INCIDENT OR ACCIDENT IN DETAIL _____

GIVE THE APPARENT CAUSE(S) OF THE INCIDENT OR ACCIDENT _____

GIVE ANY ADDITIONAL INFORMATION YOU FEEL WOULD BE HELPFUL IN DETERMINING THE CAUSE(S) OF THE INCIDENT OR ACCIDENT. _____

REPORTED BY	DATE	REVIEWED BY	DATE

The investigation of the incident itself will necessarily focus on such issues as what went wrong; whether warnings or instructions were absent, faulty, or ignored; whether proper use of the product was reviewed with the customer by the sales or service personnel; and whether the product behaved in its anticipated manner or in some unanticipated manner.

If the product behaved in an unanticipated manner, the following questions should be explored. Was the product being misused? If so, was the misuse foreseeable? Was it easy for the injured person to use the product improperly, or did he or she deliberately bypass interlocks and safety devices? If modified, who modified the product and why? Was the product maintained properly? Had it been repaired?

If required warnings or instructions were not in place or in use, what happened to them? Did the user know there were warning signs or product manuals? Would any changes in the product manual or its controls make the product easier or safer to use? Did the user "know" how to use the product and the true purpose of the product? Was the injured among the group of people expected to use the product? In sum, what were the main and contributing causes of the accident?

Other key elements of a successful approach to claims handling include:

- A defense philosophy or strategy

- Prompt and knowledgeable investigation and claims evaluation

- Proper selection and education of trial counsel

- Coordinated response to discovery

- Selection, training, and coordination of expert and factual witnesses and/or consultants

- Appointment of a spokesperson to handle the media

Types of Insurance Coverage

The risk management department can purchase coverage of two types: occurrence coverage and claims-made coverage. If occurrence coverage is purchased, insurance protection exists when timely notice of a claim is given to the carrier after the accident as long as the accident *occurred within the effective dates of the policy.* Because claims can arise long after the policy has expired, "occurrence" coverage is said to have a long tail of exposure. Asbestos and other occupational disease cases are good examples of long tails of exposure.

If claims-made coverage is purchased, insurance protection exists *when notice of a claim is made during the policy period.* Claims-made coverage covers claims made during the policy period regardless of the date of the loss. For products such as asbestos where the date of the occurrence or accident is difficult to define, the claims-made coverage may be expensive.

Product liability insurance does not ordinarily cover all persons or organizations involved with the product nor all costs of an accident. For example, the distributors, installers, and maintenance persons may not be covered. The policy may be written to cover some or all of those involved with the product in the stream of commerce (by adding a vendor's coverage clause, for example) or may list only specific groups covered.

The costs of recalling or replacing defective components or products usually are not covered. Certain defense costs are not covered. Finally, punitive damages costs are (by law) often not covered because the object of such awards is to punish the manufacturer/seller for wanton or willful misconduct.

REFERENCES

Black C. *Black's Law Dictionary*, St. Paul, MN: West Publishing Company, 1993.

Freedman W. *Product Liability for Corporate Counsels, Controllers, and Product Safety Executives*, New York: Van Nostrand Reinhold Company, 1984.

Hursh RD and HJ Bailey. *American Law of Products Liability*, 2nd edition, 6 vols., Rochester, NY: Lawyers Cooperative Publishing Company, 1974.

McGuire EP. *The Product-Safety Function: Organization and Operations*. New York: The Conference Board, Inc., 1979.

Smith CO. *Products Liability: Are You Vulnerable?* Englewood Cliffs, NJ: Prentice-Hall, Inc., 1981.

11

Product Safety Program Audits

Every good program needs a system to evaluate its continuing effectiveness. For product safety, many organizations use an audit procedure for such evaluation. This chapter outlines how to set up and conduct such an audit and includes a product safety audit checklist that can be tailored to achieve your organization's goals.

MANAGEMENT COMMITMENT

The spark that initiates the product safety program and the catalyst that provides the impetus and continuity to its effectiveness is the whole-hearted commitment and support of top management. Just as with any major program, top management often underscores its commitment to product safety by putting its support in the form of a written policy that outlines basic objectives and responsibilities within the organization.

Top management commitment must be effectively communicated to and supported by lower management levels to ensure the success of the product safety program. All key people within the business organization must know that they have an important role to play in the program and must commit the time and effort required to make the program a success. In short, all affected employees must know that the control of product losses is a key company objective.

Evaluating whether such conditions exist in a company is the first overall purpose of a product safety audit. The key indicators are demonstrated interest and effort among all involved. For example, if there is a written policy with respect to product safety, it should be widely distributed to management, just as any other important policy statement. Regardless of whether management's commitment to product safety is in the form of a written policy, the audit should expose some tangible indications of a true commitment to product safety.

TYPES OF AUDITS

Types of audits include (1) management systems audits, (2) compliance audits, and (3) awareness audits. Any of these can be done by internal or external personnel.

Product safety audits vary according to how often they are conducted and according to who does them. Some companies conduct frequent or periodic audits while others do them infrequently or on an as-needed basis. Some integrate the auditing function with day-to-day product safety operations so that audits, in effect, are accomplished in connection with the established management control system. Audits are done by an audit team that includes the product safety professional, his or her supervisor, a safety committee member, employees knowledgeable about the key issues, or by outsiders such as a consulting firm, product safety specialists from an insurance company, or a product safety department of a corporate parent or headquarters office. Audits conducted by outside personnel have an additional value in that they lend an aura of impartiality. OSHA publishes a list of nationally recognized testing laboratories that do product testing and audits.

ORGANIZATIONAL NEEDS OR GOALS

The type of audit selected should reflect organizational goals or needs, which can include any of the following:

1. Establishing uniformity and/or control among programs of various divisions or subsidiaries of large, complex organizations

2. Satisfying a perceived need for an unbiased or fresh view of a program

3. Providing assurance for management that the established program activities are effective and adequate both short-term and long-term

4. Expanding the outlook and experience of personnel through sharing of information among various segments of an organization

5. Concentrating on organization segments suspected of having a program deficiency

6. Motivating segments of the organization to action

7. Exposing those who might have new ideas or special expertise to longstanding problems

8. Serving as a back-up in case established management controls do not function as intended

PROGRAM GOALS OF AN AUDIT

The subjects the auditor will explore vary depending on what the audit is meant to accomplish for the product safety program (Figure 11–1). Most commonly, the goal is to measure performance. That is, the audit compares what the organization has done against its stated program goals. Other audits have a narrower focus, such as assessing how well the organization has evaluated its accident exposures. Another major goal of such an audit may be to provide an oversight function to make sure no major issues have been missed. Some of the major potential oversights are as follows:

- Failure to review all product designs

- Failure to identify safety-critical parts

- Inadequate manufacturing and quality control procedures

- Inadequate preparation or review of warnings and instructions

- Misleading representations of product or services

- Underestimation of the budget or time needed for product safety efforts

Product safety audits may also help generate ideas about additional steps the organization might take to improve product safety. The audit checklists provided in this chapter might serve in this capacity (Figure 11–2).

HOW TO CONDUCT THE AUDIT

Applying the technique described here will help the program auditor to achieve the goals of any type of product safety audit. In fact, this information could be incorporated as a provision of the product safety program itself.

Reviewing and tailoring the checklist in Figure 11–2 to suit the individual organization and particular audit goals forces the auditor or audit team to preplan the entire audit.

Preliminary Procedures

Prior to conducting the actual audit, the auditor, if from an outside organization or an individual not personally involved with the product safety program, should have (1) studied all information sources (as described in Chapter 1, Basic Concepts); (2) reviewed the products and potential product accident exposures; and (3) reviewed the product safety plan or program. The auditor must also do the following preliminary steps before beginning the formal audit:

- Confirm the scope and method of the audit with top management.

- Arrange mutually agreeable audit dates and review plans with appropriate members of management.

- Review appropriate documentation and procedures related to the product safety program.

- Review appropriate technical information and standards related to the products.

- Acquire a representative sample of the necessary product-related literature.

- Make sure appropriate people are available.

- Make sure incident information is available.

Obviously, the prepared auditor will tend to receive better cooperation from all involved. Cooperation is vital if the auditor is to collect the information required to evaluate program activities in the organization.

The Audit Checklist Approach

When conducting a self-audit evaluation, it is helpful to use a segmented audit checklist, such as the one in Figure 11–2. Each involved department manager is given the appropriate section of the checklist to use. The manager then answers the questions on his or her part of the checklist, giving grade rating from "A" to "C" and adding any comments. An "A" indicates that an area is fully and adequately covered. A "B" indicates that the area has many satisfactory components, but there remain practical improvements that could and should be made. A "C" implies that little control exists in this area and substantial improvements should be made, on a priority basis. A "C" grade is a warning signal that indicates a need for further evaluation and constructive plans for improvement.

The auditor then meets with each manager to discuss the manager's answers, especially those accompanied with "warning signals." The auditor solicits improvement suggestions and a timeframe for each. The auditor reviews all department responses to see if special coordination of corrective efforts is necessary. The auditor prepares a well-organized report for the appropriate level of management (either a written or oral report, depending upon management preferences) and presents it with all checklists.

AUDIT REPORT

The audit report should have an executive summary of findings as its initial section. Depending on the goals of the audit, this summary section might include the auditor's opinion of the company's overall product safety program. At times, consensus will be reached immediately about certain recommendations to correct deficiencies detected during the audit.

If recommendations are made, they must be adequately explained in the next section, the body of the report. Tentative recommendations, that is, ideas for improving safety that require further study, also belong in the body of the report.

Finally, the report should contain some sort of ranking or priority of items requiring either implementation or further study. Special provisions for follow-up response or reporting are advisable.

Figure 11–1. Possible Program Goals of a Product Safety Audit

1. Validation of product accident exposures

2. Evaluation of capability to control exposures

3. Validation of appropriate corrective measures

4. Summary of status of product safety efforts

5. Uncovering oversights

6. Comparison of what has been accomplished to what was intended to be accomplished

7. Improving product safety or accident experience

Figure 11–2.   Product Safety Self-Audit Evaluation

Product Safety Audit

_____
Unit

_____
Auditor

_____
Location

_____
Date

Item	Rating			Comments
	A	B	C	
Summary				
Management Considerations	☐	☐	☐	
Marketing Department	☐	☐	☐	
Engineering Department	☐	☐	☐	
Manufacturing Department	☐	☐	☐	
Purchasing Department	☐	☐	☐	
Quality Control Department	☐	☐	☐	

Figure 11–2. Product Safety Self-Audit Evaluation
continued

Product Safety Audit

Unit

Auditor

Location

Date

Item	Rating A	B	C	Comments

Management Consideration

1. List title of each member of Product Safety Committee.

   a. How effective are established Corporate Product Safety guidelines? ☐ ☐ ☐

   b. Are roles/responsibilities defined at all occupational levels? ☐ ☐ ☐

   c. Has a Product Safety Program been established in accordance with Corporate guidelines? ☐ ☐ ☐

   d. Has a product Safety Committee been established? ☐ ☐ ☐

   e. Are minutes and activities recorded? ☐ ☐ ☐

   f. Does the Committee develop specific annual goals? ☐ ☐ ☐

   g. Is there a written record retention program in line with Corporate guidelines (normal lifetime of products)? ☐ ☐ ☐

Figure 11–2.   Product Safety Self-Audit Evaluation
continued

Item	Rating A	B	C	Comments

Management Consideration continued

h. Does the Committee periodically review adequacy of record retention program and adherence to it by all affected departments?	☐	☐	☐	
2. Have written standards, procedures, and specifications addressed safety aspects of new product design? If yes, list the source of these documents (i.e., federal, industry, trade association, UL, etc.)	☐	☐	☐	

_____

_____

_____

| 3. Does the Unit include user safety considerations in the design of its products? If yes, by what mechanisms? | ☐ | ☐ | ☐ | |

_____

_____

_____

| 4. Does the Unit maintain records of personal injury or property damage related to its products? | ☐ | ☐ | ☐ | |
| 5. Does the Unit include product safety testing as part of its New Product Qualification Test/ Product Release procedures? | ☐ | ☐ | ☐ | |

Figure 11–2. Product Safety Self-Audit Evaluation
continued

Item	Rating A	B	C	Comments

Management Consideration continued

6. Does the Unit have the laboratory and personnel capability to perform all necessary product safety tests? If no, describe how and where these tests are performed. ☐ ☐ ☐

_____

_____

_____

7. If the Unit had to recall a part of some production run, could that portion be traced and found without recalling all of the product? Could the entire production run be recalled? ☐ ☐ ☐

8. Is there an active employee education program for product safety? Does it include all appropriate departments (Engineering, Marketing, Manufacturing, Quality Control, Service, etc.)? All levels of employees (including hourly)?

a. Are training sessions, including subject matter, date, and attendees documented? ☐ ☐ ☐

b. Is training "single shot" or "ongoing"? ☐ ☐ ☐

Figure 11–2. Product Safety Self-Audit Evaluation
continued

Product Safety Audit

Unit

Auditor

Location

Date

Item	Rating A B C	Comments

Marketing Department

1. Is sales literature describing the proper use and the limitations of the product (load, speed, environmental condition, etc.) provided to the final customer? ☐ ☐ ☐

2. Does the sales literature which is provided with the product contain all the characteristics and information regarding the product which are necessary for its safe use? ☐ ☐ ☐

3. Are safety suggestions provided? ☐ ☐ ☐

4. Is the material used in sales promotion, advertising (including information printed on packaging), and public relations reviewed by legal counsel? ☐ ☐ ☐

5. Has the literature been reviewed to remove such statements as "absolutely safe," "fool proof," "accident proof," etc.? ☐ ☐ ☐

Figure 11–2. Product Safety Self-Audit Evaluation
continued

Item	Rating			Comments
	A	**B**	**C**	

Marketing Department continued

6. Does the material contain any descriptions of the products that exaggerate its performance capabilities or suggest operations which might be dangerous for the casual user? ☐ ☐ ☐

7. Is any information pertinent to safety omitted from this material so as not to portray the product properly? ☐ ☐ ☐

8. Do promotional exhibits (photographs, sketches, diagrams, etc.) shown in sales promotion, advertising, and public relations material carefully reflect all necessary accident prevention features such as safe operating practices, proper personal protective devices, approved guarding, and so forth? ☐ ☐ ☐

9. Do these exhibits reflect safe operating conditions? If not, are adequate explanatory comments used regarding "caution," "use by experts," etc? ☐ ☐ ☐

10. Is the department aware of possible dangers from purchase orders and contracts containing hold-harmless or indemnification clauses under which the company contracts to assume liability that would normally rest on others? ☐ ☐ ☐

Figure 11–2.   Product Safety Self-Audit Evaluation
continued

Item	Rating A	B	C	Comments

Marketing Department continued

11. Are all sales personnel well informed and aware of limitations and safe use of the product? ☐ ☐ ☐

12. Is information related to accident claims issued to authorized distributors or dealers on those aspects over which they have some control? ☐ ☐ ☐

13. Do sales personnel use field service reports to record work done in servicing the product? ☐ ☐ ☐

14. If yes, do these reports also require the field representative to record any defective or unsafe conditions that he/she may observe, other than authorized service work, on the service report? ☐ ☐ ☐

15. Is the customer required to sign this report as evidence that the condition(s) has been drawn to his/her attention? ☐ ☐ ☐

16. Is there an adequate program for preserving key sales correspondence and sales records and communicating these data to other departments as required? ☐ ☐ ☐

17. Are marketing representatives and dealers properly instructed as to procedures and alternatives to follow in the event of an accident involving one of the products? ☐ ☐ ☐

Figure 11–2. Product Safety Self-Audit Evaluation
continued

Product Safety Audit

	_____
	Unit
	_____
	Auditor
	_____
	Location
	_____
	Date

Item	Rating			Comments
	A	**B**	**C**	

Engineering Department

1. Has close liaison been established among Quality Control, Engineering, Sales, Service, Safety, Manufacturing, Legal, Marketing, and Insurance Departments in the review and analysis of incidents and claims and actual accident claims? ☐ ☐ ☐

2. Has the intended use and reasonable misuse of the product been clearly established and documented? ☐ ☐ ☐

3. Does Engineering accept and understand its total responsibility for safety in the design? ☐ ☐ ☐

4. Is there a clearly written policy for this responsibility? ☐ ☐ ☐

5. Have the engineers responsible for the adequacy of the product design been properly trained and informed regarding current government policy and laws pertaining to product safety such as recent court rulings, OSHA, Consumer Product Safety Act, etc.? ☐ ☐ ☐

Figure 11–2.   Product Safety Self-Audit Evaluation
continued

Item	Rating A	B	C	Comments

Engineering Department continued

6. Does the design of the product, particularly any and all critical component parts, reflect the standards of the American National Standards Institute, Joint Industrial Conference, National Machine Tool Builders' Association, National Fire Protection Association, any other applicable national professional society or local codes, and/or the requirements of other standards-setting organizations? ☐ ☐ ☐

    a. Are approval and listing by Underwriters' Laboratories or other recognized testing or certification agencies obtained on finished product or component parts (when required)? ☐ ☐ ☐

    b. If so, are reports on file? ☐ ☐ ☐

7. Are the following records being retained for a reasonable period reflecting the expected life of the product?

    a. Organizations and societies to which the company's professional employees and any consulting firms belong? ☐ ☐ ☐

    b. Current blueprints and specifications pertaining to the product? ☐ ☐ ☐

    c. Foreseeable uses of the product? ☐ ☐ ☐

Figure 11–2. Product Safety Self-Audit Evaluation
continued

Item	Rating A	B	C	Comments

Engineering Department continued

d. Patents and patent applications? ☐ ☐ ☐

e. Identity of safety devices incorporated in and/or available for the product? ☐ ☐ ☐

f. Engineering data on all the safety factors used in the design of the product? ☐ ☐ ☐

g. Personnel records showing education, training, and Code Committee Membership of all professional personnel? ☐ ☐ ☐

h. List of information given to purchasers and ultimate users of the product (decals, plates, owner's/operator's manual, maintenance books, etc.)? ☐ ☐ ☐

i. Expert trial testimony witnesses, i.e., technically qualified and articulate? ☐ ☐ ☐

8. Are Quality Control records being utilized by Engineering for:

a. Reviewing of manufacturing discrepancies? ☐ ☐ ☐

b. Material review actions? ☐ ☐ ☐

c. Investigation and analysis of nonconforming articles and functional failures? ☐ ☐ ☐

d. Feedback for design changes and for specifying new components? ☐ ☐ ☐

Figure 11–2.   Product Safety Self-Audit Evaluation
continued

Item	Rating A B C	Comments

Engineering Department continued

9. Is the proposed advertising literature reviewed by the Engineering Department for technical accuracy or exaggerated performance statements?   ☐ ☐ ☐

10. Is the draft copy of material used in sales promotion, advertising (including information printed on packaging), and public relations reviewed by Engineering?

   a. Does the material contain any description of the product that exaggerates its performance capabilities?   ☐ ☐ ☐

   b. Is any information pertinent to liability omitted from this material so as not to portray the product properly?   ☐ ☐ ☐

   c. Do the illustrations and photographs used in this material reflect safe operating conditions?   ☐ ☐ ☐

   d. If they do not, are adequate explanations regarding caution, use by experts, etc., included?   ☐ ☐ ☐

Figure 11–2. Product Safety Self-Audit Evaluation
continued

Item	Rating A	B	C	Comments

Engineering Department continued

11. Do promotional exhibits (photographs, sketches, diagrams, etc.) shown in sales promotion, advertising, and public relations material carefully reflect all necessary accident prevention features such as safe operating practices, proper personal protective devices, approved guarding, and necessary cautionary and explanatory notes if not used in a safe manner?   ☐ ☐ ☐

12. Are formal design reviews being conducted at appropriate times and are written records kept?   ☐ ☐ ☐

13. Have provision of Items 1 through 6 of this section been included in this design review?   ☐ ☐ ☐

14. Has the expected life of the product been documented?   ☐ ☐ ☐

15. Is the designer of each critical part predicting the most likely failure modes, as a result of the necessary comprises and assumptions he or she has had to make? Is the designer documenting the fact that these failure modes are unlikely to occur under the condition of reasonable use of the product?   ☐ ☐ ☐

Figure 11–2.   Product Safety Self-Audit Evaluation
continued

Item	Rating A	B	C	Comments

Engineering Department continued

16. Does the reviewer add information as to the expected effect
of failures upon components
and subsystems? ☐ ☐ ☐

17. Does this review have rep-
resentation from the following
organizational elements:

   a. The safety professional who
has been responsible and ac-
countable for product safety? ☐ ☐ ☐

   b. Design engineering? ☐ ☐ ☐

   c. Assembly—manufacturing? ☐ ☐ ☐

   d. Tooling—manufacturing? ☐ ☐ ☐

   e. Quality control? ☐ ☐ ☐

   f. Test engineering? ☐ ☐ ☐

   g. Service? ☐ ☐ ☐

   h. Marketing? ☐ ☐ ☐

18. Has the paper design as well
as the production unit been
checked for the following human
factor considerations?

   a. Are adequate guards and
shields provided for moving
parts like chains, belts,
sprockets, cutter, fans, etc.? ☐ ☐ ☐

   b. Are there design features to
warn or dissuade users of
the product from removing
guards, shields, interlocks, or
other protective devices? ☐ ☐ ☐

Figure 11–2. Product Safety Self-Audit Evaluation
continued

Item	Rating A	B	C	Comments

Engineering Department continued

c. Are there any unprotected sharp edges on components of the product that could harm the user? ☐ ☐ ☐

d. Are there any built-in pro-visions to limit the operation of the product to the safe condition (speed control, dead-man control, electrical ground, fuses, safety valves, etc.)? ☐ ☐ ☐

e. Are there any provisions to prevent the operation or use of the product by unautho-rized persons? ☐ ☐ ☐

f. Are permanent safety warning notices affixed to the product to alert untrained users regarding potential hazards? ☐ ☐ ☐

g. Is the product safe when left unattended? If not, are there any measures taken to make the product safe when unattended? ☐ ☐ ☐

h. Are there any redundancies in critical areas of the product to secure safe operation (in brakes, mechanical lock design, electrical grounding)? ☐ ☐ ☐

i. Is rated capacity indicated on the product by means of an atattached plate, stamping, cast legend, or other perma-nent means? ☐ ☐ ☐

Figure 11–2. Product Safety Self-Audit Evaluation
continued

Item	Rating A	B	C	Comments

Engineering Department continued

j. Has consideration been given to potential secondary accidents during the expected life of the product? For example, in the design of a toy auto, if there will be deterioration of the steering wheel material during the expected life, will the wheel cause injury to the operator if he or she is thrown against the wheel by a sudden impact? ☐ ☐ ☐

k. Are all safety-critical parts clearly and permanently identified by means of a part number or coded symbol to ensure that authorized parts of the proper configuration are being used? ☐ ☐ ☐

l. Are the appropriate levels of Engineering that are responsible for the design of the product promptly notified of the failures and/or defects during manufacture, test, or use? ☐ ☐ ☐

m. Are the appropriate levels of Engineering responsible for the design of the product notified immediately of any inadequacies of components that involve human factor considerations? ☐ ☐ ☐

Figure 11–2.   Product Safety Self-Audit Evaluation
continued

Item	Rating A	B	C	Comments
Engineering Department continued				
n. Are sales and service personnel well informed and aware of limitations and safe use of the product?	☐	☐	☐	
o. If components are the product, has effective liaison been established with end-product manufacturers (to advise of safety parameters)?	☐	☐	☐	
19. Design Tests				
a. Are all relevant product safety considerations included in the product design test specifications and procedures?	☐	☐	☐	
b. Are product safety test results reported in the qualification test report?	☐	☐	☐	
c. Have the prototype, pilot, and preproduction models been tested for safety and reliability?	☐	☐	☐	
d. If so, are these reports on file?	☐	☐	☐	
e. Are there tests performed to prove the strength of the product with sufficient safety factors?	☐	☐	☐	
f. If so, are these reports on file?	☐	☐	☐	

Figure 11–2. Product Safety Self-Audit Evaluation
continued

Item	Rating A	B	C	Comments

Engineering Department continued

20. Installation/Maintenance/
Operator's/Owner's Manual

   a. Is there an operator's/
owner's manual? ☐ ☐ ☐

   b. Are the inherent hazards, if
any, in the operation of the
product pointed out and is
information given concerning
the lessening or avoidance
of the hazards? Are safety
and courtesy hints provided,
including reasonable misuse
cautions? ☐ ☐ ☐

   c. If installation is to be made
or assembly performed by
the purchaser, does the
manual stress safe methods
and practices? ☐ ☐ ☐

   d. Is the manual simple and easy
to follow? ☐ ☐ ☐

   e. Are the important assembly
operations sufficiently stressed
by underlining, bold print, etc.,
for safe and proper assembly? ☐ ☐ ☐

   f. Is it clearly defined as to
when an owner may do
repairs, etc., versus obtaining
qualified technicians? ☐ ☐ ☐

   g. Does the manual use defined
words and symbols to differ-
entiate safety messages from
maintenance, etc.? ☐ ☐ ☐

Figure 11–2.   Product Safety Self-Audit Evaluation
continued

Item	Rating A	B	C	Comments

Engineering Department continued

h. Are there clear instructions regarding care, cleaning, and maintenance of the product? ☐ ☐ ☐

21. Is the design test specification approved and reviewed periodically by Engineering? ☐ ☐ ☐

22. Are service personnel's reports on customer complaints and liability checks being used by Engineering to check the following?

a. Are safety aspects such as guards in place, etc.? ☐ ☐ ☐

b. Has the machine been altered in any way? ☐ ☐ ☐

c. Are maximum load capacities being observed? ☐ ☐ ☐

d. Incorporated in design review? ☐ ☐ ☐

e. Are servicing instructions being followed? ☐ ☐ ☐

23. Do engineering specifications for packaging meet requirements of Uniform Freight Classification (NMFC) or other recognized codes for packaging? ☐ ☐ ☐

24. Has Quality Control been supplied with a list and/or drawings of safety aspects that need to be inspected or tested? ☐ ☐ ☐

Figure 11–2. **Product Safety Self-Audit Evaluation**
continued

Product Safety Audit

	_____
	Unit
	_____
	Auditor
	_____
	Location
	_____
	Date

Item	Rating			Comments
	A	**B**	**C**	
Manufacturing Department				
1. Are all safety-critical parts of the product clearly identified by means of a coded symbol to ensure that authorized parts of the proper configurations are used?	☐	☐	☐	
2. Is the finished product free from sharp edges and corners that may be harmful when the product is handled or operated?	☐	☐	☐	
3. Are the following Quality Control records being used and communicated to all manufacturing sections who need to use these data?				
a. Distribution of manufacturing discrepancies?	☐	☐	☐	
b. Material review actions?	☐	☐	☐	
c. Investigation and analysis in regard to nonconforming articles and failures?	☐	☐	☐	

Figure 11–2. Product Safety Self-Audit Evaluation
continued

Item	Rating			Comments
	A	B	C	

Manufacturing Department continued

4. Is production equipment, including inspection/test equipment, maintained sufficiently so as to perform the specified function adequately? ☐ ☐ ☐

5. Is the work area kept clean, ventilated, and well lit, so as not to adversely affect worker or machine performance? ☐ ☐ ☐

6. Are all specifications and work instructions clear and easy to follow? ☐ ☐ ☐

7. Is supervision sufficient to ensure that specifications and work instructions are being closely followed? ☐ ☐ ☐

8. Are all materials and parts protected from damage during the manufacturing process? ☐ ☐ ☐

9. Are all finished parts and subassemblies stored in a protective manner? ☐ ☐ ☐

Figure 11–2. Product Safety Self-Audit Evaluation
continued

Item	Rating A	B	C	Comments
Manufacturing Department continued				
10. Is a current list of all blueprints and specifications pertaining to the product maintained?	☐	☐	☐	
11. Is corrective action being taken to control recurrence of discrepancies?				
a. Is the action adequate?	☐	☐	☐	
b. Is the action recorded?	☐	☐	☐	
c. Are the proper Manufacturing Departments notified?	☐	☐	☐	
12. Is packaging done according to Engineering specifications?				
a. Does packaging conform to construction requirements or other recognized codes, e.g., Uniform Freight Classification (NMFC) for packaging?	☐	☐	☐	

Figure 11–2.   Product Safety Self-Audit Evaluation
continued

Product Safety Audit

Unit _____

Auditor _____

Location _____

Date _____

Item	Rating A	B	C	Comments

Purchasing Department

1. Do purchase orders contain hold-harmless or indemnification clauses under which vendors or subcontractors might assume liability for their products and/or performance? ☐ ☐ ☐

2. Are disclaimers or warranties used with respect to products or components which are purchased or subcontracted? ☐ ☐ ☐

3. Is a current list or file of all pertinent blueprints and specifications maintained? ☐ ☐ ☐

4. Is corrective action being taken by vendors to control recurrence of discrepancies?

   a. Is the action adequate? ☐ ☐ ☐

   b. Is the action recorded? ☐ ☐ ☐

   c. Are the proper departments notified? ☐ ☐ ☐

5. Are the Quality Control requirements and Engineering specifications used in the procurement of:

Figure 11–2.   Product Safety Self-Audit Evaluation
continued

Item	Rating A	B	C	Comments

Purchasing Department continued

a. Raw materials? ☐ ☐ ☐

b. Vendor components? ☐ ☐ ☐

c. Vendor complete sub-assembly units? ☐ ☐ ☐

6. Does Quality Control verify the vendor's adequacy prior to procurement?

a. Is this done on a periodically predetermined schedule? ☐ ☐ ☐

b. Is the vendor's product marked with an acceptance tag by the vendor's Quality Control Department? ☐ ☐ ☐

7. Are all specifications and work instructions to vendors clear?

a. Is it verified that these specifications and work instructions are being closely followed by their Quality Control Department? ☐ ☐ ☐

8. Are purchased parts and assemblies packaged according to adequate specifications?

a. Does packaging of purchased parts and assemblies conform to construction requirements of Uniform Freight Classification (NMFC) or other recognized codes for packaging to prevent damage during transit and handling? ☐ ☐ ☐

Figure 11–2. Product Safety Self-Audit Evaluation
continued

Product Safety Audit

Unit _____

Auditor _____

Location _____

Date _____

Item	Rating A	B	C	Comments

Quality Control Department

1. Is there a current Quality Control Manual or specified Quality Control Program?

    a. Is it maintained and updated periodically? ☐ ☐ ☐

2. Does this manual or program include the following?

    a. Quality requirements for raw materials, vendor components, vendor complete subassembly units? ☐ ☐ ☐

    b. In-process control, including inspection and calibration of production gauges and measuring devices? ☐ ☐ ☐

    c. Requirements for Quality Control assurance of finished products? ☐ ☐ ☐

    d. Type and frequency of inspection and test? ☐ ☐ ☐

    e. Directives for documentation? ☐ ☐ ☐

    f. Professionally designed, statistically based sampling procedures? ☐ ☐ ☐

Figure 11–2. **Product Safety Self-Audit Evaluation**
continued

Item	Rating A	B	C	Comments

Quality Control Department continued

g. Are Quality Control efforts directed by a Quality Control professional? ☐ ☐ ☐

3. Are incoming materials correctly and adequately:

   a. Identified? ☐ ☐ ☐

   b. Handled? ☐ ☐ ☐

   c. Stored? ☐ ☐ ☐

   d. Reject discussed? ☐ ☐ ☐

4. Is receiving inspection using its procedures to check shipments to requirements of relevant engineering drawings and purchase orders? ☐ ☐ ☐

5. Are the required production gauges, devices, and controls:

   a. Used? ☐ ☐ ☐

   b. Periodically inspected and calibrated? ☐ ☐ ☐

   c. Stored properly? ☐ ☐ ☐

6. Are there adequate procedure controls for each phase of production? ☐ ☐ ☐

7. Is the strength of load-carrying parts, welded components, and other critical parts checked as specified? ☐ ☐ ☐

Figure 11–2. Product Safety Self-Audit Evaluation
continued

Item	Rating A	B	C	Comments

Quality Control Department continued

8. Are field complaints reviewed from the Quality Control point of view?

  a. Are field service reports used by Quality Control to record all work done when Quality Control is on a field assignment? ☐ ☐ ☐

  b. If yes, do these reports also require the Quality Control Representative to record any defective or unsafe conditions that he/she may observe, other than authorized service work, on the service report? ☐ ☐ ☐

9. Are proper steps undertaken to correct deficiency in field performance including:

  a. Notification of all departments involved? ☐ ☐ ☐

  b. Corrective action where necessary? ☐ ☐ ☐

10. Is Quality Control checking subassemblies of the product? ☐ ☐ ☐

11. Is Quality Control checking completed products?

  a. For completion of assembly? ☐ ☐ ☐

  b. For correctness of function? ☐ ☐ ☐

  c. Are guards in place? ☐ ☐ ☐

Figure 11–2. **Product Safety Self-Audit Evaluation**
continued

Item	Rating A	B	C	Comments
Quality Control Department continued				
d. Has the product been altered in any unauthorized manner?	☐	☐	☐	
e. Are maximum load capacities indicated?	☐	☐	☐	
f. Are servicing instructions being followed?	☐	☐	☐	
g. Are Quality Control personnel well informed and aware of limitations and safe use of the product?	☐	☐	☐	
h. Has the product been damaged prior to packaging?	☐	☐	☐	
12. Do Quality Control personnel know what components or product attributes are safety critical?	☐	☐	☐	
13. Are safety-critical components or product attributes given special treatment?	☐	☐	☐	
14. Is packaging done according to Engineering specifications?				
a. Is packaging checked for completeness before shipment?	☐	☐	☐	
b. Is the product properly secured within the packaging?				

Appendix 1

Product Safety and Real Property

Real property refers to land, building, building fixtures, landscaping, and underground items (e.g., plumbing, sewer, etc.) associated with real estate. The law with respect to real property is not the same as for other products, but negligence law applies in both cases. In very fundamental ways, preventing accidents with real products involves implementing the very same ideas described in the rest of this book for ordinary products.

In product safety, the duty to prevent product accidents falls primarily on the manufacturer, though vendors, dealers, retailers, and others share the duty. However, in the case of real estate construction products, the person who bears the most responsibility for safety is the general contractor. This responsibility is shared with others, such as subcontractors, the owner, the architect, and sometimes with a number of consulting engineering firms. In the case of turn-key projects (in which the contractor does all operations from design to turning over the keys of the finished project), the contractor may assume some of the legal responsibilities normally carried by subcontractors and others in the project.

COMPLETED OPERATIONS

In construction, the term "product safety" is not used. The parallel term is "completed operations." *Completed operations* means the series of actions or program to reduce or eliminate any significant hazards resulting from how construction work is executed. In addition to the personal injury risks typical for defective nonreal products, the hazards resulting from faulty design or workmanship usually include substantial property damage potentials. Completed operations losses occur after the constructed structure has been "accepted" by the owner.

It is not the intention here to describe all the knowledge necessary to completed operations personnel, as that is beyond the scope of this appendix. Instead, the intent is to outline the most important safety activities they need to consider. This appendix uses real-life case histories to illustrate what can happen when these safety activities are not performed or when they are preformed improperly.

It will be apparent from the following topic headings that there are close parallels between what is necessary to promote product safety and what is necessary to prevent completed operations disasters. It is commonly acknowledged that completed operations are considered the product safety equivalent of the building industry. Much of the detail presented for these topics earlier in this book, while not repeated here, is nevertheless applicable.

In terms of product safety controls, there are considerable differences between a manufacturer and a contractor erecting buildings. For example, a manufacturer, making a product such as a bicycle, usually has complete control of the operation, including shipping the product out of the plant. The manufacturer will normally control the conceptual and prototype development, final design, production, quality assurance, labeling, manuals, and shipping containers. Thus, the manufacturer has an advantage from the standpoint of control.

In the case of the construction industry, there can be various control patterns. For example, in the erection of a building there can be an owner, an architect, a general contractor, and possibly several subcontractors. In most cases, the architect and any specialty engineers set up the general specifications for the building. Such plans would then be submitted for bids by a general contractor, who in turn may sublet work to several subcontractors. The quality control engineer or resident engineer has a unique problem in helping to control such an operation. Obviously, on a generalized basis, the goal is to have good communications among the owner, architect, general contractor, and subcontractors.

COMPLETED OPERATIONS PROGRAM

The first objective in a completed operations safety program is the elimination or control of the hazards so that an accident does not occur. This first line of control in completed operations safety includes the following six actions. Each is illustrated by real-life case histories showing what could happen if the action is not appropriately controlled.

Perform Design Reviews

In most instances, designs and specifications are not prepared by the contractors; however, the estimators and engineers in the contractor's office should note apparent mistakes and hazards during review of these items and refer such back to the architects or engineers with appropriate comment.

Example:
A contractor bid a job to construct a sewer through an area of soft, wet ground. Although he knew from experience that the design was probably inadequate, he took the job and proceeded to build the sewer in accordance with the plans and specifications. The sewer settled and ruptured after completion. Litigation was resolved in favor of the contractor, but resulted in loss of goodwill between the contractor and the county for which the sewer was designed—the contractor's major client.

Example:
In Texas, even if the customer provides all design and builder's drawings to the contractor, the contractor is held liable for failures because he is presumed to be the expert.

Institute Controls for Design Changes

Detail or working drawings and instructions prepared by the contractor must be drafted in strict accordance with the plans and specifications supplied by the architect and/or engineer. Changes in designs or modifications of equipment should not be made in the office and on the jobsite unless they are approved by the designer or the manufacturer, and confirmed in writing. Supervision of work in the office and on the jobsite by a registered professional engineer is important if the intent of the designer is to be correctly interpreted and completed.

Example:
A one-story school building collapsed during the placing of concrete for the roof slab. Investigation revealed a discrepancy between the column spacing as shown in the architect's plans and the steel contractor's fabrication drawings. The steel contractor had attempted to compensate for the error in the field. Columns were erected slightly out of plum and holes in base plates were enlarged with a burning torch to allow shifting of column bases to match anchor bolt locations.

Example:
A contractor installed an air-conditioning/heater unit in a TV station. The owner complained of noise, so the contractor reduced the fan speed. The unit overheated during operation, causing a fire which resulted in $300,000 damage to the transmitting equipment.

Purchase Quality Materials

Good communication and clear understanding is paramount between the contractor and the supplier so that each is fully aware of the final product use and performance requirements. Each part must be concerned with the specifications, applicable codes, and related hazards affecting the completed job. In addition to the contract specifications and the local building codes, there are recognized standards published for almost every type of material and equipment intended for use in a construction project. Document that qualified people verified that the specified building materials were delivered.

Example:
A warehouse collapsed under a snowload of 25 psf, although the building has been designed to carry this load. Investigation revealed that the 40-foot-long prestressed concrete for sections had been cast using standard, heavyweight concrete, although the specifications called for the use of a lightweight aggregate. The supplier of the concrete section was in bankruptcy at the time of the roof collapse, leaving the general contractor to bear the loss alone.

Example:
Plaster was to be placed on the underside of slabs in an apartment house complex. The plasterer sprayed a chemical adhesive "lath" on the slabs and applied a 3-inch coat of white plaster to this lath. The plaster started falling soon after the job had been completed. It was determined that the adhesive was not suitable for this particular job.

Institute Quality Assurance Procedures

Good craftsmanship at the jobsite has always been the goal of the contractor. Completed operations safety control stresses this need for quality. Continuous supervision of work performance by qualified, experienced superintendents and supervisors is essential if the goal of quality assurance is to be achieved. Equipment should be installed in accordance with manufacturers' recommendations and materials in accordance with design drawings.

Example:
A collapse of a concrete structure revealed that many reinforcing bars had been omitted and those in place had been improperly spaced. The use of unskilled local labor and inadequate supervision appeared to be the cause.

Perform Design Tests and Quality Tests

System, load, and material tests and inspections are commonly required by contract specifications or are performed by the representative of the owner. The contractor should see that these requirements are performed in a careful and competent manner and that the tests and inspections required are adequate to ensure the safety of the work. If no tests are required in the specifications, a contractor should carry out his or her own tests to assure the quality of the work. Records should be kept on all tests and inspections performed.

Example:
A slip joint was installed between two sections of 10-inch piping in the pump house of a new sprinkler system. This section of piping was not pressure tested before the job was completed and turned over to the owner. The slip joint eventually moved out and up from its seating, and this movement allowed serious flooding to occur.

Example:
A piping system was installed to carry raw materials for a baking process. The system was not inspected and cleaned before being put into use. Metal shavings and filings contaminated 120,000 pounds of flour and 90,000 pounds of sugar.

Example:
A contractor installed a gas heater in a residence which had gas piping already installed, but no other gas appliances. The installer opened the cock at the meter, lit the heater, and then turned it off. Later the owner lit the heater and an explosion occurred. An uncapped gasline was discovered behind the electric stove in the kitchen. A manometer test would have revealed the gas leak.

Anticipate Foreseeable Construction Errors

Professionalism and the rules of common sense and self-interest should urge designers to try to anticipate foreseeable construction errors. Unusual or unexpected design details should preferably be highlighted on drawings by means of special views or notes. Special quality inspections may also be helpful. The architect and/or contractor should verify that the building plan details the methods of erection or installation before work is initiated.

Example:
One of the greatest tragedies of recent years that involved completed operations was the collapse of the "skywalks" at a Kansas City hotel. Over a hundred guests lost their lives. Post-accident investigations

indicated that the construction of the hangers supporting the skywalks was not in accord with the drawings and that the intended design was strong enough to support the crowds present the night of the accident. Nevertheless, the designers contributed large sums of the out-of-court settlement. Apparently, they were fearful of the argument that the intended design was time and labor intensive and the designers should have anticipated that on-site modifications to the design would likely be made.

COMMUNICATIONS FOR COMPLETED OPERATIONS

A second major objective of a safety program is to properly convey adequate information to the user. It is important that the construction contractor consider providing warnings where other safeguards are not feasible because of inherent hazards in the use or reasonably foreseeable misuse of structures or installed equipment. The user can be informed in the following three ways.

Warning Plates, Labels, Tags

The owner/user should be provided with warnings or instructional plates, labels, and tags. Warning or instructional information attached to equipment must be protected and preserved during installation so that the owner and other users will receive the information which the manufacturer intends to convey to the user. When adequate warning plates and safeguards are supplied with the equipment, the contractor should see that they are procured and properly installed.

Example:
A 10-year-old boy was electrocuted when he came in contact with high voltage. He had climbed one of two poles supporting a transformer platform located on a school playground. The transmission line contractor was held liable for failure to provide adequate warning and protection.

Owner's/Operator's Manuals

Operating and service manuals are often supplied by manufacturers of equipment provided and installed as part of the job. Such manuals contain precautionary information in addition to instructions for operating and servicing the equipment. The contractor installing the equipment has a duty to see that these manuals are transmitted to a responsible representative of the owner. Document that the manuals were transferred to the owner/operator.

As-Built Drawings

The owner should be supplied with a set of drawings of a structure as built, including electrical and mechanical systems as installed.

These drawings should clearly indicate limiting conditions affecting the safety of the structure or the system, including safety operation, loading, temperature, voltage, or pressure limits. In situations where these drawings are prepared by an architect or consulting engineer, the contractor should review the drawings to be sure they correctly represent the work completed.

Example:
During alterations on a building, a laborer drilled a hole through a floor slab, struck an electrical conductor, and was severely burned. The conductor was not located in the position that was indicated by the drawings.

CLAIMS DEFENSE

A third objective of a completed operations program is to be able to defend claims in the event of an accident. To do so, those involved with completed operations should be concerned with the following two areas.

Record Retention

When an accident occurs, records provide the first line of defense. In some cases, claims can be deterred when the claimant is presented early in the investigation with records indicating that the work was done properly. Vital records include, but are not limited to:

- Plans and specifications

- Change orders

- Material purchase orders

- Correspondence relating to work and materials

- Government and/or building inspector releases

- Progress photos and records

- Reports of all tests, including those for materials, load capacity, and equipment or system functioning

- Inspection reports by owners, architects, engineers, and public agencies

Example:
Failure of the steel frame of a six-story motel occurred two years after completion of the structure. Litigation involved the architects, the structural engineers, the fabricator, and the steel erection subcontractor.

The steel erector was severely hampered in defense because he had destroyed all drawings, specifications, and correspondence connected with job.

Conducting Accident Investigation

Accident investigation serves a two-fold purpose. First, it documents all pertinent conditions existing at the time of the accident. Second, it may reveal a means to prevent recurrence. To accomplish these purposes, company personnel should follow established, detailed procedures in all investigations.

Prompt investigation is perhaps the most important single factor determining success. The accident scene changes rapidly and memories fade. Therefore, photographs of the site and eyewitness interviews are essential to preserve a record of exact conditions immediately after the accident occurred.

Close liaison should be maintained with the insurance carrier regarding accident reporting and investigation. Any accident which might have resulted from the completed work must be promptly reported to the liability insurer. Engineers should be made available to the insurance carrier for technical assistance in the event of litigation. Rapid and complete communication between the interested parties will help establish the best defense possible.

Example:
A contracting firm completed a subcontract to install steel sheet piling at a building project site. When the piling contractor received a phone call from the general contractor stating that the sheeting had failed, he immediately advised the insurance company of the situation. A consulting engineer and a professional photographer retained by the insurance company were on the site the same day. With information obtained at the site and supplied by the piling contractor, it was possible to determine that the excavation contractor had improperly removed material securing the toe of the sheeting. The loss was accepted by the excavation contractor in an out-of-court settlement.

Whether the product is a ladder, a generator, or a building, ensuring the safety of the owner/user is a complex task. For real products, consumer products, or industrial products, the key to success is an organized and consistently applied program.

Appendix 2 Key Elements of the Consumer Product Safety Act

The following is a brief overview of the Consumer Product Safety Act with numerous amendments, the most recent being in 1990. It is not intended to be a comprehensive explanation of the Act or its many requirements. For specific information about the requirements of the Act, contact the Consumer Product Safety Commission, Washington, DC 20207.

The Consumer Product Safety Act became Public Law 92-573 on October 27, 1972, effective December 26, 1972. It has been modified numerous times, the most recent being the Consumer Product Safety Improvement Act of 1990 (PL 101-608, November 16, 1990). The Act is broad in its scope, and affects manufacturers, merchandisers, and their products that reach consumers.

The Act is complex and many of its provisions are subject to strict legal interpretation. The summary given here is intended only to highlight the key elements of the Act. For more detail, see the text of the complete Act. The information that follows has been rephrased for simplicity.

PURPOSES OF THE ACT

The purposes of the Act include:

1. Protecting the public against the unreasonable risk of injury associated with consumer products.

2. Assisting consumers in evaluating the comparative safety of consumer products.

3. Developing uniform safety standards for consumer products and minimizing conflicting state and local regulations.

4. Promoting research and investigation into the causes and prevention of product-related deaths, illnesses, and injuries.

CONSUMER PRODUCT DEFINITION

"Consumer Product" is defined as an article, or component part thereof, produced or distributed:

1. For sale to a consumer for use in or around a permanent or temporary household or residence, a school, in recreation, or otherwise.

2. For the personal use, consumption, or enjoyment of a consumer in or around a permanent or temporary household or residence, a school, in recreation, or otherwise.

Products excluded from the authority of the Act include products not normally used by consumers, tobacco and associated products, motor vehicles and associated equipment, commercial and agricultural poisons as defined in the Federal Insecticide, Fungicide and Rodenticide Act, firearms and ammunition, aircraft and associated equipment, amusement rides at fixed locations, and products already regulated under federal regulation, such as boats, boating equipment, drugs, medical devices, cosmetics, and food.

Authority is not granted the CPSC to regulate any risk of injury associated with a consumer product if it can be eliminated or reduced to a sufficient extent by actions taken under the Occupational Safety and Health Act of 1970, the Atomic Energy Act of 1954, or the Clean Air Act.

Nor does the Commission have any authority to regulate any risk of injury associated with electronic product radiation emitted from an electronic product if such risk of injury may be subject to regulation under Subpart 3 of Part F of the Title III of the Public Health Service Act.

Responsibility for the administration of the Federal Hazardous Substances Act, the Poison Prevention Packaging Act, the Flammable Fabrics Act and the Refrigerator Safety Act have been transferred to the Commission.

ADMINISTRATION OF THE ACT

The Consumer Product Safety Commission is an independent regulatory agency consisting of three Commissioners, with one of them serving as the Chairperson. Activities of the Commission involve, but are not limited to, the following:

1. Maintaining an injury information clearinghouse

2. Conducting studies and investigations of deaths, injuries, disease, other health impairments, and economic losses resulting from accidents involving consumer products

3. Conducting research, studies, and investigations covering the safety of consumer products

4. Testing consumer products and developing product safety test methods and testing devices

5. Offering training in product safety investigation and test methods and assisting public and private organizations, administratively and technically, in the development of safety standards and test methods

6. Making grants or entering into contracts to carry out its functions

7. Communicating to each manufacturer of a consumer product, insofar as it may be practical, information as to any significant risk of injury associated with a product

8. Promulgating consumer product safety standards

9. Proposing and promulgating a rule declaring that a product is a banned hazardous product

10. Holding public hearings or conducting investigations or proceedings to determine whether petitions concerning Consumer Product Safety Rules should be granted

11. Filing actions in a United States district court for seizure of an imminently hazardous consumer product

12. Issuing orders to take appropriate corrective actions after determining a product presents a substantial product hazard and that notification be made, if required, in order to adequately protect the public

13. Inspecting premises after presenting appropriate credentials and a written notice

14. Holding hearings or other inquiries necessary or appropriate to its functions

15. Initiating, prosecuting, defending, or appealing any court action in the name of the Commission for the purpose of enforcing the laws subject to its jurisdiction

16. Requiring manufacturers to provide technical data related to performance and safety to assure compliance with the Act

PUBLIC DISCLOSURE OF INFORMATION

The Commission cannot publicly release information about a product of which the manufacturer is readily identifiable without taking reasonable steps to assure the accuracy of the information. The Commission must notify the manufacturer or private labeler of a product that information about the product has been requested, and prepare a summary of the information. The Commission must also assure that the information is fair in the circumstances, and reasonably related to effectuating the purposes of the Act.

PROHIBITED ACTIONS

It is unlawful to:

1. Manufacture for sale, offer for sale, distribute in commerce, or import into the United States, any consumer product that is not in conformity with an applicable consumer product safety standard under this Act

2. Manufacture for sale, offer for sale, distribute in commerce, or import into the United States, any consumer product which has been declared a "banned hazardous product"

3. Fail or refuse to permit access to, or copying of, records; fail or refuse to make reports or provide information; fail or refuse to permit entry or inspection

4. Fail to furnish information required when a product fails to comply with an applicable consumer product safety rule or contains a defect which could create a substantial product hazard

5. Fail to comply with an order relating to notification, repair, replacement, and refund

6. Fail to furnish a required certificate, issue a false certificate if such person in exercise of due care has reason to know that such certificate is false or misleading in any material respect, or fail to comply with any rule relating to labeling

7. Fail to comply with rules relating to stockpiling

8. Fail to comply with any rule relating to provision of performance and technical data

9. Fail to comply with any rule or requirement relating to the labeling and testing of cellulose insulation

10. Fail to comply with a statement by the Commission regarding the export of either banned hazardous substances or a product not in conformance with a consumer product safety standard under this Act

11. Fail to furnish information required regarding civil actions as detailed in Section 37 of the Act

PENALTIES

Civil

Any person who engages in a prohibited act as defined and limited by the Consumer Product Safety Act is exposed to potential civil penalties, not to exceed $6,000 for each violation. Penalties imposed can be as high as $1,500,000 for a series of related activities.

Each failure to comply with the inspection of records or the reporting and entry requirements of the Act can be considered a separate violation. Additional penalties can be imposed for each failure to refuse to allow or perform any of those requirements, and each day of a continuing failure or refusal is considered a separate offense. These additional penalties can also total as much as $1,500,000.

The Commission may compromise civil penalties.

Criminal

Any person who knowingly and willfully violates any of the "prohibited acts" after having received notice of noncompliance from the Commission shall be fined not more than $50,000 or be imprisoned not more than one year, or both.

An individual director, or agent of a corporation who knowingly and willfully authorizes, orders, or performs any of the acts or practices constituting in whole or in part a violation of the "prohibited acts," and who has knowledge of notice of noncompliance received by the corporation from the Commission, shall be subject to penalties without regard to any penalties to which the corporation may be subjected.

INJUNCTIVE ENFORCEMENT

Authority is given to the United States district courts to restrain any violation of the "prohibited acts" or restrain any person from distributing in commerce a product which does not comply with a consumer product safety rule. Also, a district court action may result in the condemnation of a consumer product that fails to conform to an applicable consumer product safety rule.

PRODUCT CLASSIFICATION

Banned Hazardous Product

A rule declaring a product a "banned hazardous product" may be proposed and promulgated by the Commission when it finds that:

1. A consumer product is being, or will be sold, in commerce and the product presents an unreasonable risk of injury; and

2. No feasible consumer product safety standards under the Act would adequately protect the public from the unreasonable risk of injury associated with the product.

Specific Product Bans

The Consumer Product Safety Act bans certain specific products:

1. Butyl nitrite and related chemical mixtures;

2. Isopropyl nitrite and other nitrites; and

3. Lawn darts as specified in the Federal Hazardous Substances Act regulations.

Imminently Hazardous Consumer Products

For the purposes of the Act, the term "imminently hazardous consumer product" means a consumer product which presents imminent and unreasonable risk of death, serious illness, or severe personal injury.

An action may be filed in a United States district court by the Commission against either an imminently hazardous consumer product for seizure and condemnation or against any manufacturer, distributor, or retailer of such product, or both. This action should occur regardless of the existence of a consumer product safety rule applicable to the product. An "imminently hazardous consumer product" is subject to seizure and condemnation.

Substantial Product Hazard

After affording interested persons, including consumers and consumer organizations, an opportunity for a hearing, if the Commission determines that a product presents a "substantial product hazard," it may order that the manufacturer or any distributor or retailer of the product must take any one or more of the following actions:

1. To give public notice of the defect or failure to comply with an applicable consumer product safety standard

2. To mail notice to each person who is a manufacturer, distributor, or retailer of the product

3. To mail notice to every person to whom the product was delivered or sold, within the knowledge of the person required to give notice

It is required that notice shall immediately be given to the Commission by every manufacturer of a consumer product and every distributor and retailer of a product who obtains information which reasonably supports the conclusion that a product presents a "substantial product hazard": that is, fails to comply with an applicable consumer product safety rule; or contains a product defect which creates a substantial risk of injury to the public.

If a determination is made that a substantial product hazard exists, the Commission may order that the manufacturer, distributor or retailer of that product take one of the following actions:

1. Bring the product into conformity with the applicable consumer product safety rule or repair the defect in the product

2. Replace the product with a like or equivalent product without the defect

3. Refund the purchase price of the product (less a reasonable allowance for use if the product has been in the possession of the consumer for at least one year)

INFORMATION REPORTING REGARDING CIVIL SUITS

If a particular model of a consumer product is the subject of at least three civil actions within a twenty-four month period resulting in a final settlement for the plaintiff, the manufacturer must notify the Commission within thirty days of the settlement. The civil suits discussed here must be for death or grievous bodily injury, and they must result in a settlement or a judgement for the Plaintiff. The twenty-four month periods are specifically identified in the Act. Notification shall include:

- Name and address of the manufacturer

- Model and model number of the product involved

- Statement of death or grievous bodily injury

- Statement of the outcome of the case

- Identification of the case number and court in which the action was filed

IMPORTED AND EXPORTED PRODUCTS

Imported products must meet all the same standards as domestically produced goods. Imported products which fail to comply with existing regulations may be re-exported provided that at least 30 days before export, the importer notifies the Commission of the intent to export the products. The Commission then notifies the government of the country to which the product will be exported of the identity of the product, the reason for the denial of entry, the intended date of shipment, the quantity and port of destination, and any other required information.

DAMAGE SUITS

Only when the amount in controversy is $10,000 or more, a person who sustains injury because of a known violation of a consumer product safety rule, or any other order issued by the Commission, may sue in a district court of the United States. Remedies provided for by this part of the Act are in addition to and not in lieu of any other remedies provided by common law or under federal or state law.

Compliance with consumer product safety rules or orders shall not relieve any person from liability at common law or under state statutory law to any other person.

Failure of the Commission to take any action or commence a proceeding with respect to the safety of a consumer product shall not be admissible evidence in litigation at common law or under state statutory law relating to a consumer product.

PRIVATE ENFORCEMENT

Any interested person may bring an action in the United States district court to enforce a consumer product safety rule or an order pertaining to a "substantial product hazard" and to obtain appropriate injunctive relief. Notice to the Commission, to the Attorney General, and to the person against whom the action is directed is required not less than 30 days prior to the commencement of action.

COMMISSION PROCEDURES

Prior to promulgating a consumer product safety rule, the Commission shall consider and shall make appropriate findings for inclusion in such rule, with respect to:

1. The degree and nature of the risk of injury that the rule is designed to eliminate or reduce.

2. The approximate number of consumer products, or types or classes subject to a rule.

3. The need of the public for the consumer products subject to the rule and the probable effect of a rule upon the utility, cost, or availability of products to meet the need.

4. Any means of achieving the object of the order while minimizing adverse effects on competition, disruption, or dislocation of manufacturing and other commercial practices consistent with the public health and safety.

SAFETY STANDARDS

A consumer product safety standard is applicable only to consumer products manufactured after the effective date of the standard, which shall be at least 30 days after the date of promulgation unless the Commission, for good cause shown, determines that an earlier date is in the public interest.

A consumer product safety standard shall consist of one or more of any of the following:

1. Requirements as to performance

2. Requirements that a consumer product be marked with or accompanied by clear and adequate warnings or instruction or requirements respecting the form of warning or instructions

Any requirements of a standard shall be reasonably necessary to prevent or reduce an unreasonable risk of injury associated with a product.

JUDICIAL REVIEW AND CONGRESSIONAL VETO

Any person adversely affected by a consumer product safety rule promulgated by the Commission may file a petition with the United States District Court of Appeals for judicial review of the rule. Any petition for judicial review of a rule must be filed within 60 days of the rule being promulgated.

In addition, the Commission is required to submit a copy of any consumer product safety rule promulgated by the Commission to the Secretary of the Senate and the Clerk of the House of Representatives. Such rules will not take effect if:

1. Both Houses of Congress adopt a concurrent resolution disapproving the rule within 90 days of the continuous session of Congress; or

2. One House adopts such a resolution within 60 days and the other House does not disapprove the resolution.

STANDARDS DEVELOPMENT

A proceeding for the development of a consumer product safety standard under the Act is commenced by the publication in the *Federal Register* of a notice which shall:

1. Identify the product and the nature of the risk of injury associated with the product;

2. Include a summary of regulatory alternatives under consideration including voluntary consumer product safety standards and include information about existing standards with a summary of the reasons why the Commission believes that such standards do not eliminate or adequately reduce the risk of injury; and

3. Include an invitation for any person, including any state or federal agency (other than the Commission) within 30 days after the date of publication of the notice, to submit to the Commission an existing standard or to offer to develop the proposed safety standard.

If the Commission determines that a standard exists which has been issued or adopted by any federal agency or any other qualified agency, organization, or institution and that the standard if promulgated under the Act would eliminate or reduce the risk of injury associated with the product, then it may, rather than accept an offer to develop a standard, publish the existing standard as a proposed consumer product safety rule.

The Commission shall rely on voluntary standards rather than promulgate a mandatory standard whenever compliance with such voluntary standards would eliminate or adequately reduce the risk of injury addressed, and it is likely that there will be substantial compliance with such voluntary standards. The Commission also devises procedures to monitor compliance with such voluntary standards.

In any case, all persons interested in the standard are invited to comment. The Commission shall give interested persons an opportunity for the oral presentation of data, views, or arguments, in addition to an opportunity to make written submissions concerning the proposed consumer product safety rules.

Prior to promulgating a consumer product safety rule, the Commission shall conduct a cost-benefit analysis of the rule to determine that the benefits of the rule bear a reasonable relationship to its costs.

Appendix 3

Injuries Associated with Consumer Products

The following list of items found in and around the home was selected from the U.S. Consumer Product Safety Commission's National Electronic Injury Surveillance System (NEISS) for 1994. The NEISS estimates are calculated from a statistically representative sample of hospitals in the United States. Injury totals represent estimates of the number of hospital emergency department-treated cases nationwide associated with various products. However, product involvement may or may not be the cause of the accident.

Estimated Injuries Related to Selected Consumer Products, 1994

Product	Injuries[1]
Home Maintenance	
Cleaning equipment, noncaustic detergents	27,697
Cleaning agents (except soaps)	40,284
Paints, solvents, lubricants	21,659
Soaps, detergents	10,301
Home Workshop Equipment	
Batteries, all types	9,728
Hoists, lifts, jacks, etc.	17,555
Power home tools, except saws	35,455
Power home workshop saws	87,875
Welding, soldering, cutting tools	18,663
Wires, cords, not specified	14,221
Workshop manual tools	122,871
Yard and Garden Equipment	
Chain saws	41,474
Hand garden tools	49,349
Hatchets, axes	14,323

Estimated Injuries Related to Selected Consumer Products, 1994 continued

Product	Injuries[1]
Lawn, garden care equipment	64,778
Lawn mowers	80,712
Trimmers, small power garden tools	14,409
Other power lawn equipment	24,652
Packaging & Containers, Household	
Cans, other containers	238,476
Glass bottles, jars	60,159
Home Furnishings, Fixtures, and Accessories	
Bathroom structures, fixtures	233,079
Beds, mattresses, pillows	408,049
Carpets, rugs	128,463
Chairs, sofas, sofa beds	410,878
Desks, cabinets, shelves, racks	221,475
Electric fixtures, lamps, equipment	56,274
Holiday, party supplies	11,068
Ladders, stools	189,715
Mirrors, mirror glass	25,010
Miscellaneous decorating items	27,640
Miscellaneous household covers, fabrics	23,665
Other miscellaneous furniture, accessories	64,038
Tables, not elsewhere classified	325,975
Home Structures and Construction Materials	
Cabinet or door hardware	23,749
Ceilings, walls	253,991
Counters, counter tops	39,638
Fences	122,551
Garage doors and openers	19,656
Glass doors, windows, panels	209,884
Handrails, railings, banisters	46,422
Nails, carpet tacks, etc.	227,666
Nonglass doors, panels	329,801
Outside attached structures, materials	26,693
Porches, open side floors, etc.	133,918
Stairs, ramps, landings, floors	1,946,602
Window, door sills, frames	66,284
Housewares	
Cookware, pots, pans	28,218
Cutlery, knives, unpowered	472,085
Drinking glasses	122,464
Scissors	30,684
Small kitchen appliances	38,708
Tableware and accessories	108,242
General Household Appliances	
Cooking ranges, ovens, etc.	49,555
Irons, clothes steamers (not toys)	17,981
Refrigerators, freezers	35,098
Vacuum cleaners	16,124
Washers, dryers	19,888

Estimated Injuries Related to Selected
Consumer Products, 1994 continued

Product	Injuries[1]
Heating, Cooling, and Ventilating Equipment	
Air conditioners	12,338
Chimneys, fireplaces	23,660
Fans (except stove exhaust fans)	19,229
Heating stoves, space heaters	30,227
Pipes, heating and plumbing	29,596
Radiators	15,864
Home Communication, Entertainment, and Hobby Equipment	
Sound recording, reproducing equipment	43,470
Telephones and telephone accessories	17,453
Television sets, stands	43,313
Personal Use Items	
Cigarettes, lighters, fuel	19,771
Clothing	144,910
Grooming devices	35,371
Jewelry	54,689
Paper money, coins	27,422
Pencils, pens, desk supplies	46,939
Protection devices	13,107
Razors, shavers, razor blades	38,162
Sports & Recreation Equipment	
Amusement attractions (including rides)	15,914
All-terrain vehicles, mopeds, minibikes	125,136
Barbecue grills, stoves, equipment	14,763
Beach, picnic, camping equipment	20,313
Bicycles, accessories	604,455
Nonpowder guns, BBs, pellets	27,156
Playground equipment	266,810
Toboggans, sleds, snow disks, etc.	53,870
Trampolines	52,892
Miscellaneous Products	
Dollies, carts	47,701
Elevators, other lifts	16,807
Fireworks, flares	13,288
Gasoline and diesel fuels	20,124
Nursery equipment	108,217
Toys	160,302

Source: Consumer Product Safety Commission, National Electronic Injury Surveillance System. Reprinted from *Accident Facts*, 1996, National Safety Council.

[1] Estimated number of product-related injuries in the United States and territories that were treated in hospital emergency departments in 1994. Not all product categories are shown.

Appendix 4

CPSC Recall Handbook*

This handbook focuses on the procedures for manufacturers, importers, distributors, and retailers of consumer products to initiate corrective action programs under Section 15 of the Consumer Product Safety Act. Another Commission Office, the Division of Regulatory Management, oversees product recalls and other actions where products are believed to be in violation of government regulations or standards. Companies reporting to the Commission should first communicate with the Division of Corrective actions (301/504-0608), which will determine the appropriate office to handle the report or inquiry.

The U.S. Consumer Product Safety Commission (CPSC) is an independent regulatory agency charged with reducing unreasonable risks of injury associated with consumer products. The CPSC has jurisdiction over approximately 15,000 types of consumer products used in and around the home, in schools, and in recreation.

This handbook has been developed to familiarize companies with their reporting requirements under the Consumer Product Safety Act of 1972, as amended. This information will not only help a company recognize potentially hazardous consumer products at an early stage, but it will also assist firms in developing and implementing a "corrective action plan" to eliminate a product hazard should it exist. This handbook does not replace the Commission Statutes or Commission Interpretative Regulations which are set out in 16 CFR Part 1115. . . .

*A guide for manufacturers, importers, distributors, and retailers on reporting under Section 15 of the Consumer Product Safety Act and preparing for, initiating, and implementing product safety recalls. U.S. Consumer Product Safety Commission, Directorate for Compliance and Administrative Litigation, Division of Corrective Actions, Washington, DC 20207, Telephone: 301–504–0608, October 1988.

For more information about reporting requirements, see also the Commission's Statement of Enforcement Policy, 51 *FR* 23,410 (1986).

The term "corrective action plan" (CAP) is used to describe any type of corrective action measure taken by a firm. It could be a recall and return of the product to the manufacturer, importer, distributor, or retailer. Or, it could be a product warning. Likewise, it could involve the repair of the product by the consumer, retailer, or manufacturer; the exchange of the product for a product without the defect; or a cash refund of the purchase price.

This handbook is expressly written for manufacturers, private labelers, importers, distributors, and retailers who produce and/or distribute consumer products that fall within the jurisdiction of the U.S. Consumer Product Safety Commission. The handbook, however, is not an all-inclusive reference source for the recalling of products. If firms are faced with recalling a product and developing a corrective action program, the Commission encourages these firms to be creative in their recall efforts, so as to retrieve as many hazardous products from the distribution chain and from consumers as possible in the most feasible manner. By working closely with Commission staff in developing specific corrective action plans to correct unsafe products, the public will be protected.

I.
REPORTING REQUIREMENTS

Section 15(b) of the Consumer Product Safety Act (CPSA) 15 U.S.C. § 2064(b), defines responsibilities of manufacturers, importers, distributors, and retailers of consumer products. Each is required to notify the Commission if it believes (1) a product fails to meet a consumer product safety standard or banning regulation, or (2) a product has a defect which could create a substantial hazard to consumers. The Commission's interpretive regulation (issued in August 1978 under section 15 of the CPSA, Substantial Product Hazard Reports, 16 *CFR* Part 1115) explains the company's obligations and those of the Commission. Companies that distribute consumer products that fall under the provisions of the Flammable Fabrics Act, the Federal Hazardous Substances Act, the Poison Prevention Packaging Act, the Refrigerator Safety Act, and the Consumer Product Safety Act must comply with these reporting requirements.

The intent of Congress in enacting section 15(b) of the CPSA was to encourage widespread reporting of potential product hazards. Congress sought not only to have the Commission uncover substantial product hazards, but also to identify risks of injury which the Commission could attempt to prevent through its own efforts, such as information and education programs, safety labeling, and adoption of product safety standards. Although the agency relies on sources other than company reports to identify substantial product hazards, reporting by companies under section 15 provisions is invaluable because firms often learn of product safety problems long before the Commission does. For this reason, any company involved in the manufacture, importation, distribution, or sale of consumer products should develop a system of reviewing and maintaining consumer complaints, inquiries, product liability suits, and comments on the products they handle.

If a firm reports to the Commission under section 15 of the CPSA, it does not necessarily mean there is a substantial product hazard. Section 15 simply requires firms to report whenever a product fails to comply with consumer product safety rules and/or contains a defect that could create a substantial product hazard. Thus, a product need not actually create a substantial product hazard to trigger the reporting requirement.

A.
When to Report

It is the Commission's view that a firm should take that all important first step of notifying the Commission when the information available to the company reasonably indicates there is a product defect which could create a substantial product hazard or that the product fails to comply with a standard or banning regulation issued under the CPSA. If a product fails to comply with a regulation issued under the Flammable Fabrics Act, Federal Hazardous Substances Act, Poison Prevention Packaging Act, or Refrigerator Safety Act, the firm must report if that failure to comply results in the product having a defect that could create a substantial product hazard.

It is in the company's interest to assign the responsibility of reporting to someone in executive authority. That individual's knowledge of the product and the reporting requirements of section 15 are valid reasons for delegating responsibility. Part 1115 of the Commission's regulations interpreting the reporting requirements, . . . provide guidelines for companies to use in determining whether a product defect exists.

B.
Confidentiality of Reports

The Commission often receives requests for information provided by firms under section 15(b) of the CPSA. Section 6(b) of the CPSA, 15 U.S.C. § 2055(b)(5), prohibits the release of such information unless a remedial action plan has been accepted in writing, a complaint has been issued, or a firm consents to the release. Firms submitting information considered to be a trade secret, confidential commercial or financial, must mark it "confidential" in accordance with section 6(a)(3) of the CPSA. If a firm does not request confidential treatment at the time of its submission of information, or within ten days thereafter, the CPSC staff will assume that the firm does not consider the material in its submission to be a trade secret or otherwise exempt from disclosure under section 6(a) of the CPSA and the Freedom of Information Act, 5 U.S.C. § 522(b)(4).

II.
IDENTIFYING A DEFECT

A defect could be the result of a manufacturing or production error, or it could result from the design of, or the materials used in, the product. A defect could also occur in a product's contents, construction, finish, packaging, warnings, and/or instructions.

Not all products that present a risk of injury are defective. A kitchen knife is one such example. The fact that the blade is sharp to allow the consumer to cut or slice food is the very reason why the product was created; the knife's cutting ability is certainly not a product defect, even though some consumers may cut themselves while wielding the knife.

In determining whether a product's risk of injury is the type that could make the product defective, the Commission considers the following:

1. What is the utility of the product? What is it supposed to do?

2. What is the nature of the injury that the product might cause? The kitchen knife is supposed to have a handle so you can use the knife safely; if the knife has no handle and you have to grip the cutting edge to use the knife, this could constitute a possible defect.

3. What is the need for the product? Could you possibly cut food without a knife?

4. What is the population exposed to the product and its risk of injury?

5. What is the Commission's experience with the product?

6. Finally, what other information sheds light on the product and its pattern of consumer use?

If the information available to the company does not reasonably support the conclusion that a defect exists, the firm need not report to the Commission. However, since a product may be defective even if it is designed, manufactured, and marketed exactly as intended, the company should report if it is in doubt as to whether a defect exists.

If the information obtained by the company supports a conclusion that the product has a defect, the company must then consider whether the defect is serious enough that it could create a substantial product hazard. Generally, a product presents a substantial hazard when consumers are exposed to a significant number of units or if the possible injury is serious or is likely to occur. Because most companies seldom know the extent of public exposure or the severity of the injury when a product defect first comes to their attention, the company should report to the Commission even if they don't know whether a substantial product hazard exists.

Section 15 lists the statutory criteria for determining a substantial product hazard, including the pattern of defect, the volume of defective products distributed in commerce, and the severity of the risk to consumers. Any one of the following factors could indicate the existence of a substantial product hazard:

1. Pattern of defect. The defect may stem from the design, composition, content, construction, finish, packaging, warnings, and/or instructions accompanying the product. Or, conditions may exist under which the defect presents itself.

2. Number of defective products distributed in commerce. A single defective product could be the basis for a substantial product hazard determination if an injury is likely or could be serious. By contrast, a few defective products posing no risk of serious injury and having little chance of causing even minor injury, ordinarily would not be considered to present a substantial product hazard.

3. Severity of risk. A risk is considered severe if the injury that might occur is serious or likely to occur. Likelihood of injury is determined by considering the number of injuries which have occurred, the intended or reasonably foreseeable use or misuse of the product, and the population group exposed to the product (such as children, the elderly, and the handicapped).

A substantial product hazard may exist when a product does not comply with an applicable consumer product safety rule, provided this lack of compliance creates a substantial risk of injury to consumers.

A. Company Reports

A company is considered to have knowledge of product safety information when such information is received by an employee or official of the firm who may reasonably be expected to be capable of appreciating the significance of that information. Under ordinary circumstances, five (5) days is the maximum reasonable time for that information to reach the chief executive officer or other official assigned responsibility for complying with the reporting requirements. Weekends and holidays are not counted in that timetable.

The Commission will evaluate whether or when a firm should have reported. This evaluation will be based, in part, on what a reasonable person, acting under the circumstances, knows about the hazard posed by the product. Thus, a firm shall be deemed to know what it would have known if it had exercised due care ascertaining the accuracy of complaints or other representations.

A company should report to the Commission under section 15 within 24 hours of obtaining information which reasonably supports the conclusion that a product does not comply with a product safety rule or contains a defect which possibly could create a substantial risk of injury to the public. The company may report a substantial product hazard to the Commission even while its own product investigation is continuing.

If the company is uncertain as to whether the information is reportable, the firm may elect to spend a reasonable time investigating the matter, but no evaluation should exceed ten (10) days unless the firm can demonstrate that a longer timetable for the investigation is reasonable. If a firm elects to conduct an investigation to decide whether it has reportable information, the Commission will deem that, at the end of ten (10) days, the firm has received and considered all information which would have been available to it had a reasonable, expeditious, and diligent investigation been undertaken.

B. Information to Be Reported

A company calling the Commission (301–504–0608) to report a potentially defective product should be prepared to provide some general and background information; however, no company should delay its report because some of the vital information has not been compiled. The following information should be transmitted to the Commission by telephone:

• Description of the product

• Name and address of your company, whether you are a manufacturer, distributor, importer, or retailer

• Nature and extent of the possible product defect

• Nature and extent of injury associated with the product

• Name, address, and telephone number of the person informing the Commission

• To the extent such information is reasonably available, the data specified in Section 1115.13(d) of the Commission's regulations interpreting the reporting requirements

C.
Retailer and Distributor Reporting

Retailers and distributors may satisfy their reporting obligations under section 15 either by telephone (301–504–0608) or by writing the Division of Corrective Actions, Directorate for Compliance and Administrative Litigation, U.S. Consumer Product Safety Commission, Washington, DC 20207. Alternatively, the retailer or distributor may transmit a letter to the manufacturer or importer describing the defective or non-complying product and forward a copy of that letter to the Division of Corrective Actions at the address listed above. Retailers and distributors also must report information received from another firm about a defective or non-complying product handled by the retailer or distributor. Similarly, a distributor or retailer receiving product hazard information from a manufacturer or importer should report to the Commission unless the manufacturer/importer advises that the CPSC has already been notified.

III.
CPSC RECEIPT OF SECTION 15 REPORTS

When a company reports to the Commission about a possible product defect, the Division of Corrective actions (located within the Directorate for Compliance and Administrative Litigation) undertakes the same product hazard analysis as that requested of firms. First, a preliminary decision is made as to the presence of a defect in the product. If the Division staff believes there is a defect, an assessment is made as to the substantial product risk presented to the public. Using the same criteria as applies to companies (that is, pattern of defect, number of defective products distributed in commerce, severity of the risk, and other appropriate data), the Division staff then applies hazard priority standards to classify the severity of the problem. This hazard priority system is also used to guide the Corrective Actions staff in selecting the level and intensity of the corrective action program that the company will be asked to undertake if, indeed, the staff decides that a substantial product hazard exists.

IV.
HAZARD PRIORITY SYSTEM

The hazard priority system allows the Commission staff to rank defective products uniformly. For example, a Class A hazard rating is reserved for product defects where there is a strong likelihood of death or grievous injury or illness to the consumer.

Regardless of whether a product defect is classified as a Class A, B, or C priority hazard, the common element among these defects is that each of them presents a substantial product hazard and corrective action must be undertaken to reduce that risk of injury.

A.
Class A Hazard

- Exists when a risk of death or grievous injury or illness is likely or very likely, or serious injury or illness is very likely.

Class A hazards warrant the highest level of company and CPSC attention. They call for immediate, comprehensive, and imaginative corrective action measures by the company, such as identifying consumers having the defective product and advising them of what steps to take to remedy the problem. Such corrective action measures would include, but are not limited to, the following:

- Maximum direct notice to the product distribution network

- Maximum direct notice to consumers or groups who have or use the product. This notice could include one or more of the following communication channels:

  A joint news release issued by the CPSC and the company;

  Purchase of mailing lists of suspected product owners;

  Use of "bill stuffer" enclosures;

  Paid advertisements in nationally and/or regionally distributed newspapers and magazines reaching suspected owners of the product;

Installation of an "800" toll-free telephone line to receive calls from consumers having the defective product;

Using incentives such as "bounty" money, gifts, and premiums to prompt consumers, distributors, and retailers to return the product;

Point-of-purchase posters at retail outlets and service centers to alert consumers to a product recall;

Use of product warranty cards or other owner information, such as rebate return cards or service contract names to identify users of the product;

Using product catalogs, marketing newsletters, or sales materials to publicize the product recall; and,

Notification to groups and trade associations for whom the product recall may have particular concern.

**B.
Class B Hazard**

- Exists when a risk of death or grievous injury or illness is not likely to occur, but is possible, or when serious injury or illness is likely, or moderate injury or illness is very likely.

This hazard priority warrants the second highest level of product recall. Efforts should be made to reach owners and users of defective products through one or more of the following:

A joint news release from the CPSC and the company;

If available, direct notice to consumers owning the product by means of warranty cards, catalog names, etc.;

Paid notices in newspapers and specialty magazines to reach targeted users of the product;

Point-of-purchase posters in retail outlets and service centers to alert consumers who may have the product;

Incentives for consumers, distributors, and retailers to return the product;

Installation of an "800" toll-free telephone line to receive calls from consumers with the product.

C.
Class C Hazard

- Exists when a risk of serious injury or illness is not likely, but is possible, or when moderate injury or illness is or is not likely, but is possible.

This level of hazard concerns products that present a less serious risk of injury than products in the previous two categories, but still warrant a recall. Since a substantial risk of injury is presented, the following resources are among those that should be used to reach consumers having such products:

A joint news release from the CPSC and the company;

If available, direct notice to consumers owning the product by means of warranty cards, catalog names, etc.;

Point-of-purchase posters in retail outlets and service centers to alert consumers who may have the product;

Notice to distributors and retailers about the product recall;

Installation of an "800" toll-free telephone line to receive calls from consumers with the product.

For recalls of products presenting Class A, B, and C priority hazards, these elements serve as guidelines for companies to use in communicating information to owners and users of the defective product. While some companies have exemplary track records with regard to communicating with consumers, it still works to a company's advantage to work with the Commission staff to use both the company's and the Commission's skills and resources for the product recall.

V.
HOW A COMPANY UNDERTAKES A PRODUCT RECALL

The objectives of a recall are:

1. To locate as quickly as possible all defective products;

2. To remove defective products from the distribution chain and to retrieve them from the possession of consumers; and

3. To communicate accurate and understandable information to the public about the product defect, the consumer hazards, and the corrective action plan.

Once the CPSC's Division of Corrective Actions staff preliminarily determines there is a product defect of substantial risk to consumers, it will seek from the appropriate firm—be it manufacturer, importer or, in some cases, private labeler, distributor, and/or retailer—the submission of a voluntary corrective action plan. This plan, which is reviewed by the Commission staff for its adequacy, then forms the basis for any action the company wishes to take to resolve the problem. In any event, it should address each of the elements cited in section 1115.20(a) of the Substantial Product Hazard Report regulations.

A.
Notification Elements

Each communication effort used by the company in the product recall must be agreed upon in advance by the Division staff. It is, therefore, very important for firms sending notifications out to customers/consumers to provide advance copies in draft form to the Division staff.

Here are some specific suggestions for communicating recall messages:

1. Notices to consumers, distributors, and retailers:

• Letters or other forms of communication should be specific and concise.

• The words "Important Safety Notice" or a heading such as "Recall Notice" should appear in the lower left hand corner of the envelope and at the beginning of each letter.

• The letter or communique should state that the recall is for safety reasons.

• The nature of the product defect or hazard, as well as the recommended action for the consumer, distributor, or retailer, should be contained in the letter.

• The letter should be individualized for the target audience (one letter for consumers, a different letter for distributors, yet another for retailers).

2. Point-of-Purchase Posters

• Posters and counter cards should be printed in colors that contrast with the background of the poster or counter card.

• Posters and counter cards should be readily visible and not blocked from consumers' view by other signs or products being sold. The message should also be easily understandable for consumers.

- Posters and counter cards should be readily displayed in several conspicuous locations throughout the store. Locations include: on the shelf where the product was routinely sold, at checkout counters and customer service desks, and at the entrance and exit to the store.

- Posters may fit standard store display holders. Ideally, posters should be no less than 22 by 28 inches to be most visible to shoppers.

- Counter cards may also fit standard display holders. Ideally, cards should be no less than 11 by 19 inches.

3. Press Releases

Unless a company can identify all purchasers of a product being recalled for direct notice, the Commission will seek to issue a press release jointly with the firm. Such releases are made available to the national wire services (AP and UPI), major metropolitan daily newspapers, television and radio networks, and periodicals on the agency's press contact mailing list.

Prepared in conjunction with the Commission's Office of Information and Public Affairs, the draft release is sent to the company for verification of content. Usually, the release from the Commission generates the widest media attention and consumer response.

In some cases, companies involved in a product recall may prefer to issue their own (unilateral) press release. However, this tends to complicate matters since the government is also releasing the news release and it could create confusion among the public.

Each product recall press release agreed to or unilaterally issued must contain the following information:

- Name of the product, the manufacturer, and the specific product hazard

- Suggested retail price of the product

- Description of the product and its intended use

- Model and serial number of the product, and where consumers will find the data on the product

- Dates and time periods of product availability, distribution, and sales to assist consumers in determining if they bought the product

- Guidelines for discontinuing use of the product, if applicable

- Directions as to how consumers may obtain refunds, replacement, or repair of the product

- Major national stores or chains selling the product

- Description of the defect and the date the Commission was first notified of its existence

- Name and "800" telephone number for consumers to use if they wish to contact the company with questions about the recall

A glossy, black-and-white photograph or line drawing from the company showing the product and the defect is also recommended; duplicating the photograph and/or line drawing and providing it to the media with the release usually eliminates any confusion and often resolves their questions.

Companies whose products come under the jurisdiction of the CPSC should consider developing an organizational policy and plan in the event a product recall or similar action becomes necessary, whether it involves the CPSC or another government agency. This policy and related plans should focus on the early detection of product safety problems.

VI.
DEVELOPING A COMPANY POLICY AND PLAN TO IDENTIFY DEFECTIVE PRODUCTS AND TO UNDERTAKE A PRODUCT RECALL

A.
Designating a Recall Coordinator

Designating a company official or employee to serve as a "recall coordinator" is one step firms can take in meeting their product safety and defect reporting responsibilities. Ideally, this recall coordinator would have full authority to coordinate all recalls, and have the sanction and support of the firm's chief executive officer.

The recall coordinator should have the following qualifications and responsibilities:

- Knowledge of the statutory authority and recall procedures of the Consumer Product Safety Commission

- Ability to function as the central coordinator within the company for all information regarding quality control procedures, product safety, and consumer complaints

- Keeping the company's chief executive officer informed about all potential product recalls and reporting requirements

- Making recommendations, as needed, about initiating product recalls

- Authority to involve appropriate departments and offices of the firm in implementing a product recall

- Responsibility for serving as the company's primary liaison person with CPSC

B.
Role of the Recall Coordinator

How can a "recall coordinator" contribute to the overall operation of the company while still being dedicated to the reporting of potential substantial product hazards? There are diverse ways in which this can be accomplished.

At the outset, the recall coordinator should fully review the company's product line to determine how each product will perform and fail under conditions of proper use and foreseeable misuse or abuse. Through research and analysis, product safety engineers can identify the safety features that could be incorporated into the product to reduce its potential for future injury.

The company should institute a product identification system if one is not now in existence. Model numbers and date-of-manufacture codes should be used on all products whether they carry the company's name or are privately labeled for other firms. In the event a product recall is necessary, the company can easily identify all affected products without undertaking a costly recall of the entire production run. Similarly, once a particular type of product has been recalled and corrected, a new model number or other means of identification should be used on new non-defective products so distributors, retailers, and consumers can readily distinguish products subject to recall from those new, non-affected items.

Some companies have used stickers to identify products which have been checked and corrected from the recalled products until a production change could be made to incorporate a new model number or date code.

C.
Preparing for a
Product Recall

It is unlikely that any two recall programs will ever be identical. Therefore, companies should be prepared to address the problems that invariably arise, such as:

- What is the defect that causes the product hazard?

- What caused the product defect to occur in the first place?

- Where are the unsafe products? How many are there?

- How did the product fail to comply with government safety regulations?

- Was the government or the ruling regulatory body informed about this lack of compliance?

- Have consumers, distributors, and retailers been told about the defective products?

- Has the company discontinued production and shipments of these products to distributors?

- Has a press release been prepared dealing with the recall?

- Is the company prepared to address the legal questions concerning the defective product and any resultant injuries to consumers therefrom?

- What is the company's estimate as to the cost of the product recall campaign?

- Is the company prepared to deploy manpower and fund the effort to provide replacement parts for defective products or to exchange them for new products which do not have the problem?

- Has a plan been developed to ship replacement parts or new units to distributors participating in the product recall?

- Is the company prepared to monitor the product recall and provide timely reports to the regulatory agency on the progress of the recall?

- How is the company upgrading its quality control or risk analysis procedures to prevent a similar product recall in the future?

This list addresses most administrative and operational functions of a company involved in a product recall. Even if a company never incurs a product recall, it should be prepared, nonetheless, to respond to the questions listed above.

VII.
RECORD
MAINTENANCE

How well a company undertakes a product recall largely depends on how effectively it gathers the information needed for the recall. This points out the obvious need for maintaining accurate records about the design, production, distribution, and marketing of each company product during its expected life. Generally speaking, the following records are essential for a company to conduct an effective product recall:

1. Production records. Accurate data should be kept on all production runs, volume of units manufactured, lot numbers and product codes, component parts, and other pertinent information which will help the company identify defective products quickly.

2. Distribution records. Data should be maintained as to the location of each product according to product line, production run, quantities shipped, dates of delivery, and quantities sold to retailers.

3. Quality control records. It is to the company's benefit to maintain records documenting the results of quality control testing and evaluation associated with each production run. If the company were confronted with a product recall, these records would help identify possible flaws in the design or production of the product. It would also aid the firm in charting the appropriate corrective action plan.

4. Complaint record. Complaints from users or others in the distribution chain can be a key source of information in that they may highlight or anticipate problems which may arise in the future. Careful analysis of complaints may reveal a flaw in the product long before the product is involved in serious injuries, perhaps forcing the company into a costly recall program.

Product complaints serve as an "early warning system" and should not be ignored. Instead, they should be thoroughly evaluated to determine what prompted the complaint.

The goal of any product recall is to communicate accurate and useful information to consumers, as soon as possible, who have the potentially harmful product in their possession. The recall seeks to retrieve, repair, or replace those products already in consumers' hands as well as those in the distribution chain. Therefore, it is essential that firms have documented procedures for locating, collecting, and repairing these defective products.

VIII. CONCLUSION

Consumers no longer view product recalls in a negative light. Many thousands of products have been recalled over the years. Today, consumers believe they enjoy a safer, better product as a result of a recall. How well a company conducts a timely, reasonable recall of a product it produced can have a strong influence on the consumer's attitude about the firm. Successful product recalls in the past have often rewarded companies with continuing consumer support and demand for the firms' products.

Appendix 5 # Glossary

Note:
The following are not legal definitions, but were written for nonlawyers by contributors. If legal use is required, consult an attorney in the applicable jurisdiction.

ANSI

American National Standards Institute, a nonprofit organization, dedicated to the preparation and publication of safety guidelines for manufacturers, contractors, consumers, and the general public. It is one of the national clearinghouses and coordinating bodies for standards activity in the United States.

Class Action

A suit brought by one or more named plaintiffs as representatives of unnamed plaintiffs who are claimed to be similarly situated. The named defendants may be sued as representatives of a class of unnamed defendants who are alleged to be similarly at fault.

Completed Operations

A form of product liability coverage applicable to contractors and service organizations. It covers the insured for injuries or damage for which they may be liable after work has been completed and they have left the jobsite.

Contract

An agreement between two or more parties in which each agrees to perform some action or make payment in exchange for some action or payment by the other. Contracts may encompass other agreements (if not prohibited by statute), such as Indemnity Agreements, Hold-Harmless Agreements, etc., which can impose liabilities on a manufacturer or seller in addition to those that would be imposed by common law.

Critical Parts

Components or parts that affect safety for the intended life of the product; failure of a critical part would result in serious bodily injury, property damage, interruption of business, or serious degradation of product performance.

Deposition

The taking of pertinent testimony, not in court, but under oath in the presence of plaintiff and defense attorneys. The deposed person may be anyone having knowledge of the plaintiff's injury or the allegedly defective product in question. The testimony is intended for discovery and/or preservation of evidence.

Discovery

Investigation into the facts of a claim and/or the alleged proximate cause of injury. Discovery may include interrogatories, depositions, expert examination of the product in question, plaintiff's medical history, etc.

Ergonomics

The science of designing the job and the workplace to fit the worker. The goal of ergonomics is to allow work to be done without undue stress.

Hazard

A condition that is prerequisite to a mishap. In product safety, a real or potential condition or characteristic of a product that presents a risk of injury or damage to property. Examples: a forklift truck without overhead guard or load backrest; an unguarded power saw without an anti-kickback device; a toxic chemical; an unguarded power START button.

Hold-Harmless Agreements

A contract under which partial or total legal liability for one party is assumed by another party.

Interrogatories

A series of formal written questions served by either party to a legal action on the adversary for the purpose of discovery. The questions must be pertinent to the case and must be answered, except where objected to by counsel for legal cause. Such questions and answers are normally filed with the trial court. They can be used at the trial, especially for impeachment purposes.

Liability

The state of being bound or obliged in law to do, pay, or make good something. In tort law, liability is usually based on negligence. Products liability is usually based on the doctrine of strict liability.

Named Insured's Products

Goods or products manufactured, sold, handled, or distributed by the named insured or by others trading under the insured's name.

Negligence

Failure to act as a reasonably prudent person would act under the same circumstances. In a product liability case, negligence may be proved by showing that a reasonable manufacturer, distributor, or seller *would have done* something to improve product safety that the manufacturer, distributor, or seller in the particular case *did not do*; or that a reasonable manufacturer, distributor, or seller *would not have done* something that the particular manufacturer, distributor, or seller *did do*.

NEISS

National Electronic Injury Surveillance System collects data from 119 representative hospital emergency rooms on product-related injuries receiving emergency treatment. Data represent an estimated 38% of all product-related injuries. Since May 14, 1973, NEISS has been the Consumer Product Safety Commission's primary tool for collecting statistical injury data upon which the CPSC can base its policies and operational decisions. (See Appendix 3.)

Privity of Contract

The relationship that exists between two or more contracting parties.

Product Liability

The legal liability imposed upon a supplier of a product (manufacturer, assembler of parts, wholesaler, retailer, lessor, or other middleman) for injuries or damages to the consumer/user caused by the supplier's negligence, breach of warranty, or strict liability in tort. Simple failure of a product to perform (assuming there is no personal injury or property damage) is considered a commercial loss and is generally uninsurable.

Product Liability Insurance

Provides that the insurance company will pay on behalf of the insured all sums (within the limits of the policy) which the insured is legally obligated to pay as damages for bodily injury or property damage covered by the policy. There are two types of product liability insurance:

Occurrence coverage:
If occurrence coverage is purchased, insurance protection exists when timely notice of a claim is given to the carrier after the accident as long as the accident *occurred within the effective dates of the policy.* Because claims can arise long after the policy has expired, "occurrence" coverage is said to have a long tail of exposure. Asbestos and other occupational disease cases are good examples of long tails of exposure.

Claims-made coverage:
If claims-made coverage is purchased, insurance protection exists *when notice of a claim is made during the policy period.* Claims-made coverage covers claims made during the policy period regardless of the date of the loss. For products such as asbestos where the date of the occurrence or accident is difficult to define, the claims-made coverage may be expensive.

Punitive Damages

Damages awarded against a person or company as punishment for deliberate or reckless conduct. Such damages are intended to act as a deterrent and as a punishment to the wrongdoer.

Reasonable Care

The degree of care a person of ordinary prudence would take to avoid accidents or protect against what usually happens or is likely to happen.

Reasonably Prudent Person

The reasonably prudent person is one who acts in ordinary or usual ways; one whose actions are suitable, fit, or appropriate to the end in view. This concept, also known as the "reasonable man doctrine," applies only to negligence issues, not to strict liability.

Recall

The manufacturer's withdrawal of suspected deficient or defective products from the market or from use for inspection, repair, or replacement. Product liability insurance will not ordinarily pay for recalls. Recall endorsements, if purchased, will merely help in the process of getting the products returned to the insured.

Risk	The probability that a hazard will result in some magnitude of injury, illness, or other loss.
Self-Insured	A generic, loosely used term indicating that smaller claims are defended and/or settled by the manufacturer directly, without drawing on insurance coverage. In almost all such arrangements, however, some form of insurance coverage is involved to deal with larger claims. More properly referred to as a deductible or retention.
Service	Useful labor that does not produce a tangible product.
State of the Art	The level of technology that is demonstrably achievable without new or additional scientific research and with commercially available components and materials.
Statute of Limitations	A time limitation in which the plaintiff must file a court action. This varies by state, but generally it is a longer period for a contract action than for a negligence action. For example, in Pennsylvania, a person who is injured and bases the action on negligence, must file the suit within two years from the date of the injury, or be forever barred from filing legal action. If the action is based on contract, the time limitation is six years. A breach of warranty action is, in effect, a breach of contract; therefore, the six-year statute would apply. Many states have extended the time limit further by saying that the statute of limitations starts to run when the plaintiff first discovers that there is a probability of a casual connection between an injury and a product, even though the suspected connection is discovered years after the initial injury.
Statute of Response	A limitation of the time from the date of manufacture or sale of product during which a user can sue for injury by that product. The time varies by state from four to 12 years, but there may be a provision for certain extenuating circumstances. Relatively few states have a statute of response.

Strict Liability
The imposition of liability for damages resulting from any and all defective and hazardous products without requiring proof of negligence. Disclaimers are not valid; traditional warranty concepts, privity, and notice of injury are eliminated.

Third-Party Action
A lawsuit in which a defendant who has been sued for damages makes a claim that another individual or business (the "third party") is actually responsible for the loss and should pay any legal liability the defendant may have.

Tort
A civil wrong, other than breach of contract, for which the law allows compensation by payment of money damages.

Tortfeasor
A wrongdoer; one who is guilty of a tort or wrong.

Unreasonably Dangerous
Dangerous to an extent or in a way not reasonably expected by a buyer or user.

Vendor's Coverage
An endorsement to an insurance policy by which a manufacturer's insurance carrier agrees to provide coverage for distributors and sellers for any liability caused by the manufacturer's products.

Warranty Disclaimer
A specific denial of responsibility for liability arising out of use of a product or services performed, improperly performed, or not performed on a product; often unenforceable.

Warranty, Expressed
A statement, written or oral, by the seller to the purchaser that the product or service meets certain specifications. This is usually in writing in the form of a guarantee, which may be used for restricting liability as well as for affirmations. The definition has been broadened to include advertisements and sales literature where specific claims are made for the quality or performance of a service or product.

Warranty of Fitness Implied

An understanding between the supplier and purchaser/user that a product or service is reasonably fit for the intended use. When a service or product is purchased for a specific purpose and an organization or individual undertakes to provide this service or product, it is held that there is a valid assumption on the part of the purchaser that the product or service will be reasonably fit for the intended use. Also, where the purchaser is led to purchase the goods or services by the seller's description of them, it has been concluded that the purchaser has a right to expect the product or service to be accurately represented by the seller. Thus an unexpected, unusual, or abnormal hazard involving the seller's product or service would constitute a breach of implied warranty. The term *unexpected* is so broadly interpreted that it is difficult to define.

Appendix **6** # References

Aerospace Materials Information Center (AMIC), Air Force Materials Laboratory, Wright-Patterson AFB, OH 45433.

Aerospace Safety Research and Data Institute, NASA-Lewis Research Center, 21000 Brook Park Road, Cleveland, OH 44135.

American National Standards Institute, 11 West 42nd Street, New York, NY 10036.
>   *Accident Prevention Tags (for Temporary Hazards).*
>   ANSI Z535.5–1991.
>   *Criteria for Safety Symbols.* ANSI Z535.3–1991
>   *Environmental and Facility Safety Signs.* ANSI Z535.2–1991.
>   *Product Safety Signs and Labels.* ANSI Z535.4–1991.
>   *Safety Color Code.* ANSI Z535.1–1991.

American Society for Testing and Materials, 1916 Race Street, Philadelphia, PA 19103. "End Use and Consumer Products." *Annual Book of ASTM Standards*, 46.

Bass, L. *Products Liability: Design and Manufacturing Defects.* New York: McGraw-Hill Book Company, 1986.

Black, HC. *Black's Law Dictionary.* St. Paul: West Publishing Company, latest edition.

Canavan, MM. *Product Liability for Supervisors and Managers.* Reston, VA: Reston Publishing Company, Inc., 1981.

Consumer Product Safety Commission. *Recall Handbook.* Washington, DC: Government Printing Office, 1988.

Defense Ceramic Information Center, Battelle Memorial Institute, 505 King Avenue, Columbus, OH 43201.

Defense Metals Information Center (DMIC), Battelle Memorial Institute, 505 King Avenue, Columbus, OH 43201.

Dhillon, BS. *Human Reliability with Human Factors*. Elmsford, NY: Pergamon Press, 1986.

Eads, G, and P. Reuter. *Designing Safer Products: Corporate Responses to Product Liability Law and Regulation*. Santa Monica, CA: The Rand Corporation, 1983.

Electronic Component Reliabiliity Center (ECRC), Battelle Memorial Institute, 505 King Avenue, Columbus, OH 43201.

Epstein, RA. *Modern Products Liability Law*. Westport, CT: Quorum Books, 1980.

Failure Rate Data System (FERADA), Navy Fleet Missile Systems Analysis and Evaluation Group, Corona, CA 91720.

FMC Corporation. *Product Safety Signs and Labels*. 2d Edition. Santa Clara, CA: FMC Corporation, 1978.

Freedman, W. *Products Liability for Corporate Counsels, Controllers, and Product Safety Executives*. New York: Van Nostrand Reinhold Company, 1984.

Government-Industry Data Exchange Program (GIDEP). GIDEP Operations Center. Corona, CA 91720.

Guide to Record Retention Requirements. In *Code of Federal Regulations*. Washington, DC: Superintendent of Documents, U.S. Government Printing Office, Revised January 1, 1993.

Hammer, W. *Product Safety Management and Engineering*. 2d Edition. DesPlaines, IL: ASSE, 1993.

_____. *Handbook of System and Product Safety*. Englewood Cliffs, NJ: Prentice Hall, Inc., 1972.

International Organization for Standardization (ISO). *Safety Colours and Safety Signs*. Geneva: ISO Draft Standard, DIS 3864.3, ISO/TC80, 1978.

Kolb, J and Ross, S. *Product Safety and Liability*. New York: McGraw-Hill Book Company, 1980.

Mechanical Component Reliability Center (MCRC), Battelle Memorial Institute, 505 King Avenue, Columbus, OH 43201.

National Safety Council, 1121 Spring Lake Drive, Itasca, IL 60143-3201.
   Product Safety Reference Notes.
   Product Safety Up-to-Date.

National Technical Information Service, U.S. Department of Commerce, Springfield, VA 22151.

Placards and Labels, Title 49. *Code of Federal Regulations,* Parts 100-199. Washington, DC: Government Printing Office.

Product Liability Letter. Washington Business Information, National Press Building, Washington, DC 20045.

Product Liability Reports. Commerce Clearing House, 4025 W. Peterson Avenue, Chicago, IL 60645.

Product Safety and Liability Reporter. Bureau of National Affairs, Inc., 1231 25th Street NW, Washington, DC 20037.

Roland, HE. and Brian Moriarity. *System Safety Engineering Management,* 2d Edition. New York: John Wiley & Sons, Inc., 1990.

Salvendy, G, ed. *Handbook of Human Factors.* New York: John Wiley and Sons, 1987.

Seiden, RM. *Product Safety Engineering for Managers: A Practical Handbook and Guide.* Prentice-Hall, Inc., 1984.

Triodyne, Inc., 5950 W. Touhy, Niles, IL 60648.

Triodyne Safety Briefs, especially:
   "On Classification of Safeguard Devices (Part I),"
   vol. 1, no. 1, April 1981.
   "On Classification of Safeguard Devices (Part II),"
   vol. 1, no. 2, Sept. 1981.
   "Philosophical Aspects of Dangerous Safety Systems,"
   vol. 1, no. 4, Dec. 1982.
   "Safety Hierachy," vol. 3, no. 2, June 1985.
   "The Dependency Hypothesis (Part I)," vol. 2, no. 3, Nov. 1983.
   "The Dependency Hypothesis (Part II—Expected Use),"
   vol. 3, no. 1, Dec. 1984.

Underwriters Laboratories, Inc., 333 Pfingsten Road, Northbrook, IL 60062.
 Standards for Safety Catalog.

U.S. Army Human Engineering Laboratory, Redstone Arsenal, AL 35809.
 Human Factors Engineering Design for Army Material, (MIL-HDBK-759), 1975.

U.S. Consumer Product Safety Commission. Washington, DC 20207.

Weinstein, AS, et. al. *Products Liability and the Reasonably Safe Product: A Guide for Management, Design, and Marketing.* New York: John Wiley and Sons, 1978.

Witherell, CE. *How to Avoid Products Liability Lawsuits and Damages: Practical Guidelines for Engineers and Manufacturers.* Park Ridge, NJ: Noyes Publications, 1985.

Index